T0312274

# Cambridge Elements ☰

Elements in Public and Nonprofit Administration
edited by
Andrew Whitford
*University of Georgia*
Robert Christensen
*Brigham Young University*

# REDEFINING DEVELOPMENT

## *Resolving Complex Challenges in a Global Context*

Second Edition

### Jessica Kritz
*Georgetown University*

Shaftesbury Road, Cambridge CB2 8EA, United Kingdom

One Liberty Plaza, 20th Floor, New York, NY 10006, USA

477 Williamstown Road, Port Melbourne, VIC 3207, Australia

314–321, 3rd Floor, Plot 3, Splendor Forum, Jasola District Centre,
New Delhi – 110025, India

103 Penang Road, #05–06/07, Visioncrest Commercial, Singapore 238467

Cambridge University Press is part of Cambridge University Press & Assessment,
a department of the University of Cambridge.

We share the University's mission to contribute to society through the pursuit of
education, learning and research at the highest international levels of excellence.

www.cambridge.org
Information on this title: www.cambridge.org/9781009394864

DOI: 10.1017/9781009394833

First published 2020
Second edition 2023

*A catalogue record for this publication is available from the British Library.*

ISBN 978-1-009-39486-4 Paperback
ISSN 2515-4303 (online)
ISSN 2515-429X (print)

Additional resources for this publication at www.cambridge.org/Kritz_2nd_edition

# Redefining Development

## Resolving Complex Challenges in a Global Context

### Second Edition

Elements in Public and Nonprofit Administration

DOI: 10.1017/9781009394833
First published online: June 2020

Jessica Kritz
*Georgetown University*

**Author for correspondence:** Jessica Kritz, jessica.kritz@georgetown.edu

**Abstract:** In 2015, Old Fadama, the largest informal community in Accra, was a government "no-go zone." Armed guards accompanied a participatory action research team and stakeholders as they began an empirical research project. Their goals were to resolve wicked problems, advance collaboration theory, and provide direct services to vulnerable beneficiaries. In three years, they designed a collaboration intervention based on rigorous evidence, Ghana's culture, and data from 300 core stakeholders. Sanitation policy change transformed the community, and the government began to collaborate freely. By 2022, the intervention was replicated in Accra, Kumasi, and eleven rural communities, providing health services to more than 10,000 kayayei (women head porters) and addressing complex challenges for 15,000 direct and hundreds of thousands of indirect beneficiaries. This collaboration intervention improved community participation, changed policy, and redefined development in theory and practice. This title is also available as Open Access on Cambridge Core.

**Keywords:** cross-sector collaboration, international development, complex challenges, Africa, participatory action research

ISBNs: 9781009394864 (PB), 9781009394833 (OC)
ISSNs: 2515-4303 (online), 2515-429X (print)

# Contents

# 1 Introduction

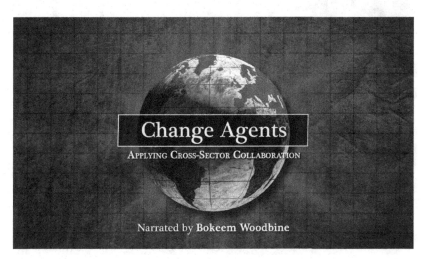

**Video 1** Change agents: Applying cross-sector collaboration. Video available at www.cambridge.org/Kritz_2nd_edition

Every urban slum creates challenges too complex for governments to resolve when working alone. Old Fadama, an informal settlement in Accra, Ghana, was established in the 1980s by migrants fleeing tribal violence in the north. It has grown steadily with spikes for a variety of reasons, including a period of intense domestic conflict in 1994 and drought conditions in 2015. Home to 79,684 residents when last enumerated in 2009 (Farouk & Owusu, 2012), in 2015 the Accra municipal government estimated that the number of residents expanded to 150,000. These included long-term settlers and multigenerational families as well as seasonal migrants coming from throughout the country. These short-term residents were motivated by regular crop cycles to sell produce at the nearby Agbogbloshie green market. Others sought access to health care, education, or work. Many Old Fadama residents did not speak English or the local languages in Accra.

Old Fadama had virtually no water or sanitation infrastructure (see Figure 1), so excreta were collected in plastic bags and disposed of in the river that bordered the slum, creating heavy silting in the nearby Korle Lagoon. Residents infilled the lagoon – packing the banks with car chassis, refuse, and sawdust – to create space for additional housing, which in turn led to flooding that spread fecal matter to the nearby Agbogbloshie market, the largest green market in the city. This cycle led to frequent outbreaks of cholera that spread throughout the country, resulting in hundreds of deaths. By 2015, when the research director for this project identified stakeholders who selected Old Fadama as a complex challenge they would like to

**Figure 1** Old Fadama informal settlement, May 2017

address, the slum – which was locally known as "Sodom and Gomorrah" – was a government "no-go zone" due to the generally lawless environment.

In the words of the director of public health (2007–2016) of the Accra Metropolitan Assembly (AMA, the mayor's office), Simpson A. Boateng, MD:

> Sodom and Gomorrah was not meant for human habitation, and all attempts to remove the people failed. It was an unorganized community; for example, there were no sanitation facilities, and there were illegal electrical connections that were fire hazards. I wanted to enter the cross-sector collaboration to help improve the conditions and standard of living. And there was a need to collaborate effectively with the community in order to achieve something. The project provided an environment for the Ghana Health Service, judiciary, police, and other stakeholders to meet so that we could discuss the problems that were confronted.
>
> My main priorities were to make sure every individual felt safe, physically and mentally. The public health department was set up to support public health in Accra by protecting the environment, food safety, making sure the food vendors were clean and making safe food for people, and ensuring sanitation policies by making sure everyone had a toilet in their home. Lack of toilets is a major problem and results in people defecating into plastic bags and throwing them into the streets and nearby river. (Gold, Audra. Q&A with Dr. Simpson A. Boateng, the former Director of Public Health, Accra Metropolitan Assembly (posted June 4, 2018), available at https://jphmpdirect.com/2018/06/04/qa-simp son-boateng/)

In February 2015, Boateng was frustrated by the repeated cholera crises that began in Old Fadama and swept throughout the city and the country. When approached by the research director for this project, he leaped at the opportunity to create a cross-sector collaboration with the community.

Grand challenges require grand strategies. In cases such as Old Fadama, no one sector – including government – can address the complex development challenges. Complex challenges are largely social, affecting many people, systems, and sectors (Rittel & Webber, 1973). They can seem difficult or impossible to resolve, and typical top-down intervention strategies are not sufficient. Cross-sector collaboration, incorporating multiple stakeholders and viewpoints, is necessary to create effective solutions.

Cross-sector collaboration occurs when governments, nongovernmental organizations, communities, and citizens come together to achieve more than they could if they worked alone (Bryson, Crosby, & Stone, 2006). These diverse entities must collaborate effectively to impact complex challenges. In the United States and Europe, collaboration research has expanded dramatically over the past fifteen years, improving the practice and the way Western governments function (Bryson, Crosby, & Stone, 2015). There are many well-developed examples of how the evidence base has been woven into the fabric of developed-country governance.

In low- and middle-income countries, many international development projects involve complex challenges, with multiple stakeholders representing various, sometimes competing, interests (Kritz, 2018). However, collaboration research is not widely conducted, and in practice, governments and international development programs have not effectively adopted collaboration tools. Consequently, complex challenges in developing countries are being addressed without the advances of this new, yet robust, field. Development researchers agree that rigorous approaches to development are badly needed (e.g., Ostrom, 2014). This Element reports such a rigorous project – an exploratory project, created in 2015 to respond to the critical evidence gap around cross-sector collaboration. The research director's goal was to develop an evidence-based, stakeholder-driven participatory action research (PAR) intervention that resolved complex challenges in Old Fadama, could be evaluated at the process level, and had the potential to be scaled up sustainably. The intervention was subsequently piloted in 2018–2019 and replicated in 2020–2022.

In PAR, researchers and participants work together to define problems and formulate research questions and solutions (Cornwall & Jewkes, 1995). This research method couples knowledge generation – such as would occur in traditional research – with an additional component: a process to create or support organizational action and change (Cornwall & Jewkes, 1995; Greenwood & Levin, 1998). Counter to the typical international development approach, in the concept phase this PAR project required the stakeholders to resource their own participation and make all the strategy decisions by consensus, including where to work and what projects to undertake: to create their own solutions for the problems they wanted to resolve. For this project, the term "stakeholders" is used to mean the local group of research participants and others (who were not research participants, usually because the research team believed saturation was reached) who saw themselves as people who had a "stake" in resolving the challenge Old Fadama was facing. With this novel approach, the initial research questions included the following:

1. Would stakeholders around a complex challenge in Ghana build a cross-sector collaboration, if invited to do so (but not provided the resources to do so, other than a facilitator and a research director to help them)?
   a. What would the stakeholders need from a facilitator?
   b. What was the role of the research director (who was not providing resources or making decisions about the direction of the project)?
2. How would the stakeholders identify a challenge?
   a. Which stakeholders would be involved in that decision making? Why?
   b. What kind of challenge would they choose (e.g., would they choose "low-hanging fruit" or would they choose to work on something more difficult)?
3. Would the stakeholders expand the collaboration? And if so, how?
   a. Would the stakeholders contribute resources to the collaboration? And if so, what?
   b. Would the stakeholders take actions to resolve the challenge they identified? And if so, who would take them? What actions would they take?

When the research director for this project approached Boateng, he immediately saw the potential that this kind of research might improve his office's results in Old Fadama. The Old Fadama collaboration began with three research participants: Boateng; his officer-in-charge for Old Fadama, Imoro Toyibu; and Sr. Matilda Sorkpor, HDR, a Ghanaian Catholic sister who worked to build a bridge between the government and the community. Peter Batsa, a researcher and project manager for the National Catholic Health Service, was engaged as a facilitator and to collect data on the project. Boateng described the beginning as follows:

> We were able to start approaching the community by involving a community health officer, Imoro Toyibu. He was from the Sodom and Gomorrah community and trained in environmental health in northern Ghana. I had just hired him … and I was excited to have a link into the community. He led us into the community and convinced the people (because he was one of them) to enter into conversations with the government [and this project's research director].
>
> The project had the full political support of the former mayor and current mayor, as well as the new Minister of Sanitation. The Sodom and Gomorrah community was fierce and violent and did not trust the government at all; it was a no-go area. This is because the government made a lot of promises that were not

fulfilled. The people also felt insecure because they thought the government was bent on getting them out of the area they occupied. (Gold, Audra. Q&A with Dr. Simpson A. Boateng, the former Director of Public Health, Accra Metropolitan Assembly (posted June 4, 2018), available at https://jphmpdirect .com/2018/06/04/qa-simpson-boateng/)

In June 2015, heavy flooding that killed hundreds of people in Accra was attributed to Old Fadama, and the AMA bulldozed the portion of the settlement that was encroaching on the river. The media captured images of violence and signs such as "Before 2016 You'll See 'Buku Harm' [Boko Haram] In Ghana." Residents rioted in response to having their homes demolished. In July 2015, the AMA hosted the first meeting with community leaders, facilitated by Batsa. As Boateng described:

We had a meeting in my office with Imoro, the Catholic Sisters, and the community leaders. This first meeting was very tense, but, gradually, they have become our friends. Normally, the AMA would make a decision and impose it on the people. The cross-sector collaborations approach involved everybody and made them part of the decision-making process; therefore, they see it as their own. And the government showed good faith and inclusiveness by coming to the meetings and discussing the projects with the community. That is one reason why this project is working.

Also, including the Catholic Sisters helped because they are respected and are seen as leaders. As I've mentioned, the community had a high level of mistrust of the government, but including the Catholics and involving the community in the initiative allowed for an effective collaboration. And it is working very well. (Gold, Audra. Q&A with Dr. Simpson A. Boateng, the former Director of Public Health, Accra Metropolitan Assembly (posted June 4, 2018), available at https:// jphmpdirect.com/2018/06/04/qa-simpson-boateng/)

**Video 2** Partners in government agencies. Video available at www.cambridge .org/Kritz_2nd_edition

From the beginning, the stakeholders expressed their frustration with short-term international development interventions that took time and resources from the community, but "nothing changed." They shared a different perspective that cut across technical sectors. They took a challenge-focused approach, and their goal was to address the root cause of the challenges facing the settlement. In this heavily conflicted environment, with the fear of AMA bulldozers, a government policy against slum upgrading, and ongoing resettlement efforts that led to violence, the early stakeholders exhibited significant courage in joining this research study.

The PAR proceeded as follows: the research director introduced the concept of cross-sector collaboration and trained Batsa on the evidence base and how to serve as facilitator. They were the research team and worked with the initial research participants in a purposive, consensus-based process to expand the collaboration. In an iterative process, the research team continued to introduce the concept of cross-sector collaboration and educate the stakeholders about the existing evidence. The stakeholders used the evidence to inform their decision making – either to validate their decisions or, when they departed from the evidence base, as a prompt to explain to the research team why they were doing so. This PAR process created a "stakeholder platform," a forum for discussions between different stakeholders to identify and prioritize community issues and develop solutions (Figure 2). The PAR process taught participants to stand in the shoes of others, learn from one another, develop a shared understanding of the challenge, and work together.

**Figure 2** Stakeholder meeting

As the collaboration took shape, the PAR process continuously expanded the number of participants. The process allowed government officials to interface with the chiefs – the tribal elders – of sixteen tribes of Old Fadama. Through a series of focus group discussions (FGDs), the research participants identified numerous priorities: sanitation, community violence, the need to support vulnerable populations of kayayei women who carry goods in the markets (typically balanced on their heads), solid waste management, and a clinic. Their first priority, sanitation, led to a sanitation strategy and latrine and bathhouse project.

A local Catholic sister, Sr. Rita Ann Kusi, HDR, joined the research team as community liaison, and she and Batsa worked with community leaders (chiefs and others) to conduct a community survey of fifty-nine research participants to expand the community stakeholders and design a public latrine and bathhouse project. The latrine and bathhouse installation created a local policy change, and this is where the results became surprising: local sanitation businesses learned of the project, saw it as workable, and wanted to participate in the policy change. On their own initiative and with their own resources, the businesses began to install latrines and bathhouses in Old Fadama, creating a path to local sustainability and freeing the stakeholders to address the next priorities, creating new strategies and projects.

This Element describes in detail how the PAR process expanded the number of stakeholders from three to three hundred research participants. The initial results are consolidated into a PAR intervention that incorporates results from the process as well as the stakeholders' first strategy, sanitation, and project, latrine and bathhouse installation. The Element then describes how the PAR process was replicated multiple times, creating novel results on a low budget and presenting new avenues for resolving complex challenges in Ghana. This Element is organized as follows.

Section 2 describes the robust field of cross-sector collaboration in developed countries, and the nascent evidence from developing countries. This section highlights and synthesizes the evidence to explain the interdisciplinary research approach to create a model for addressing complex challenges – the challenges of Old Fadama – at their root cause.

Section 3 contains the research context, including a brief historical, political, environmental, and social description of Old Fadama. The PAR methods and results of each PAR phase are described in detail.

Section 4 presents a flowchart of the PAR intervention and an evaluation of PAR as a tool for creating and supporting cross-sector collaboration. The section also explains how the latrine installation project shaped the collaboration process.

Section 5 discusses the continued work of the collaboration, 2018–2022. Stakeholder decision making about the additional priorities (community violence, solid waste management, and a clinic) was used to refine the PAR intervention and plan network analysis.

Section 6, the Conclusion, describes the theoretical and policy significance of this project, and how the process will be further scaled with government support.

## 2 Why Cross-sector Collaboration?

Cross-sector collaboration occurs when governments, nongovernmental organizations (NGOs), communities, and citizens come together to achieve more than they could if they worked alone (Bryson, Crosby, & Stone, 2006). Challenging to research and practice, this sort of collaboration is recommended when there is a clear advantage to be gained, for example, when complex challenges have defeated sectoral efforts (Bryson, Crosby, & Stone, 2015). In 2015, the Old Fadama informal settlement of Accra presented just such an environment. Boateng had already identified many sectoral international development projects that had failed. Waste-picking machines installed by an international NGO at the nearby e-waste dump were unused (see Figure 3). Repeated cholera outbreaks were traced to the slum. Large infrastructure development projects in northern Ghana failed to attract Old Fadama residents back to their homes and communities of origin. Boateng attributed these failures to the fact that they were all sectoral approaches. The cholera epidemic was a driving force for the stakeholders to take a new approach: to create a process for addressing Old Fadama's complex challenges at their root.

### 2.1 Complex Challenges

In the United States and Europe, the study of complex challenges began in the 1970s, when they were characterized as "wicked problems" (Rittel & Webber, 1973). These challenges are recognizable by their seemingly contradictory requirements, with complex interdependencies that take significant time and sustained effort even to define. Rittel and Webber (1973) transformed the thinking with the idea that a formulation of these kinds of problems was, necessarily, the solution to these problems, because the solution creation is what leads to definition. The leadership literature describes complex challenges as "adaptive" – because of their complexity, stakeholders may not only perceive the solutions differently but may even have difficulty agreeing on the problem (Heifetz, 1994).

**Figure 3** View of Old Fadama and municipal and e-waste dump

By contrast, Rittel and Webber (1973) identified "tame" challenges as those that a manager, who had the right education and competencies, could understand and solve through a formulaic process. The leadership literature calls these "technical" challenges, those that groups or a technical community would perceive and tend to design a solution the same way (Heifetz, 1994).

According to Rittel and Webber and Heifetz, understanding complex challenges comes through a deep knowledge of context, and the context is used to give the problem scope and to understand what solutions are possible. Solutions are best identified according to individual and group interests, values, and ideologies through a process involving multiple parties who are equipped, interested, and able to create the solutions.

## 2.2 Cross-sector Collaboration

The study of complex challenges evolved into the study of cross-sector collaboration. This new field began to develop rapidly in 2006, aided by an important literature review by Bryson, Crosby, and Stone that coalesced the fragmentary evidence from many disciplines into a picture catapulting the research funding and interest at the municipal, state, and federal levels in the United States. They defined cross-sector collaboration as "the linking or sharing of information, resources, activities, and capabilities by organizations in two or more sectors to achieve jointly an outcome that could not be achieved by organizations in one sector separately" (Bryson, Crosby, & Stone, 2006, p. 44). They structured their review around a number of "propositions" that they constructed based on their own research, weaving the nascent evidence from multiple fields into a picture that was accessible to both researchers and practitioners.

In 2015, this team published an updated review explaining the evolution of the field and how this research and practice, although challenging, vastly improved the way that governments – and other collaborating partners – respond to public challenges in developed countries (Bryson, Crosby, & Stone, 2015). They identified seven holistic theoretical frameworks created in the prior ten years and honed important concepts, such as design, strategic management, and governance, that had come about during that time. Elaborating on the theme that diverse entities must collaborate effectively to impact and ultimately resolve complex challenges, the review identified a number of important areas for future research focus.

Even though their review specifically excluded developing-country evidence, looking at the developed-country progress offers new avenues for thinking about how to implement the research and practice of cross-sector collaboration in developing countries. However, even with such a comprehensive and inspiring review as a starting point, when this project began, it was difficult to see how the results could be applied in Ghana. For example, one influential case study, used to advance the theory and practice, involved a $1.1 billion demonstration project to reduce congestion on an urban transportation corridor in Minneapolis, Minnesota (Bryson et al., 2011b). This funding implies a level of infrastructure and human resources that does not exist in developing countries. This resource disparity explains why it is challenging to apply the collaboration literature in developing countries and points to, perhaps, why development industry norms have not yet evolved to incorporate collaboration best practices.

## 2.3 Development as Usual

Debate among critics and proponents of international development funding has been focused on whether, or the extent to which, international aid funding and development programs should exist (Flint & zu Natrup, 2019). Critical works such as Damisa Moyo's *Dead Aid* demand an end to aid, arguing that it exacerbates poverty (Moyo, 2010). Academic Jeffrey Sachs champions the other side of the debate in *The End of Poverty: Economic Possibilities for Our Time* – that aid can transform developing economies (Sachs, 2006). Some argue development programs should exist but adapt, taking into account evidence from social capital theory (Woolcock & Narayan, 2000). Others advocate reducing overall aid and point to alternatives like social entrepreneurship and civic innovation (Fowler, 2000). The debate continues, with general agreement that current aid-funded programs do not achieve desired results, and vast improvements are needed if these systems are to end poverty (Easterly, 2008). This project started with the premise that international development programs lack efficacy and fail to become sustainable because international development funding mechanisms and projects do not take into account the evidence base on how to resolve complex challenges.

While international development models call for work across sectors, development agencies – and therefore their grantees, including researchers and practitioners – have not yet adapted to incorporating best practices from cross-sector collaboration literature and cases. Virtually every development funding agency operates with a sectoral approach, requiring proposals around predetermined issues and preferencing predesigned projects with established metrics. These factors fail to account for the human relationships (Eyben, 2010) and conflicts that must be worked through to resolve complex challenges. Thus, complex challenges are not – and cannot be – addressed effectively.

Few, if any, funders offer the flexibility of a stakeholder-driven, strategic approach that is suitable for actually resolving complex challenges. Compounding this issue, funders hinder the time-consuming process of creating sustainable solutions by imposing short timelines for reporting results (Airing & Teegarden, 2012). Thus, when development researchers or practitioners try to address complex challenges and at the same time attempt to complete their predefined program of work within a standard three- or five-year funding cycle, they run into the issue of deadlines. How would one manage the relationships and the necessary conflict that arise in the resolution of these challenges? It is not possible. Instead, the researchers and practitioners try to "tame" the "wicked" problems (to use Rittel's and Webber's language), defaulting to outdated evidence as they treat these problems as standard projects. This approach is designed to fail.

Alternatively, they may try to conduct evidence-based cross-sector collaboration, but on a shortened timeline, thus resorting to practices that are rigid, lack rigor, and misapply or do not use current evidence. In the implementation literature, this is called "rival framing"; for purposes of this discussion, it means that performance measurements and donor reports distort the activity – the work of collaboration – to comply with desired new collaboration norms (Kritz, 2017). In one glaring example, dozens of articles touted the efficacy of a major international collaboration with the laudable goal of treating and preventing HIV/AIDS in Botswana. Yet, when local stakeholders were later interviewed, researchers discovered that the Dutch project leader worked extensively in South Africa but lacked cultural competence in Botswana. The top-down approach did not readily incorporate practices that would work locally, and project results were prioritized over relationships. It took several years for the project to achieve some "mutuality" so that local government leaders believed they were valued partners (Ramiah & Reich, 2006). These issues were compounded by enormous external pressure due to short funding timelines.

Cross-sector collaboration research is needed to improve these sorts of international development programs. A more robust, contextually relevant evidence base could identify collectivist cultures that are more suited to collaboration, available resources, personnel, government structures, key jobs for international and donor organizations, and many other opportunities. This research would strengthen relationships and ultimately improve program results. This project was developed in part to address these issues.

## 2.4 Cross-sector Collaboration Evidence in Developing Countries

This research began with a literature review of the developing-country cross-sector collaboration evidence. The goals of the review were to find out how collaboration research was conducted in developing countries and to identify collaboration interventions that could be used as a model for Old Fadama.

The literature search began with health literature, which is robust and particularly well organized. A broadly constructed search identified 20,000 articles mentioning collaboration-related topics in their title or abstract. However, only 165 articles contained data on how cross-sector collaboration was implemented, and just a handful of those articles included rigorous study of the collaboration itself (Kritz, 2017). Because of the lack of evidence, the review then incorporated an extensive hand search in a number of other fields, yielding little additional data. Thus, the most important outcome from the review was to illustrate how little rigorous collaboration process research has been done in developing countries.

Nonetheless, the results, described in Figure 4 were interesting in that they explained how contextual factors differed in developing countries, while generally mirroring the developed-country theory. Thus, the results related to how to construct collaboration process were organized around the Bryson, Crosby, and Stone team's themes of design, strategic management, and governance (Bryson, Crosby, & Stone, 2006, 2015; Stone, Crosby, & Bryson, 2013).

Analyzing the results of the review combined theoretical understanding and empirical evidence and focused on explaining the relationship between the context, mechanisms, and outcomes (Pawson et al., 2005). Regarding how to conduct the collaboration research, the small number of research studies that

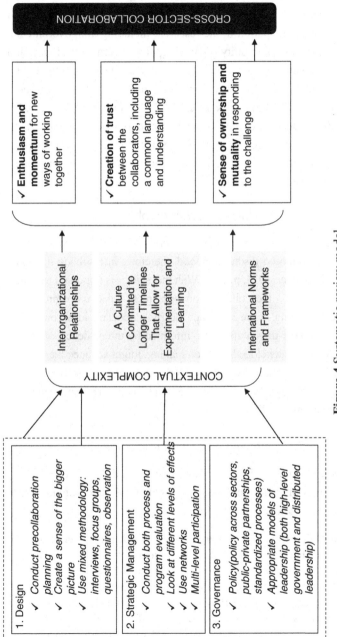

**Figure 4** Systematic review model

were deemed to be rigorous had several commonalities that were used to construct this project (Kritz, 2017). The studies (1) used mixed methodology including interviews, focus groups, questionnaires, and observation; (2) incorporated a high degree of contextual complexity into the research design; (3) involved multi-level participation in the research, including nongovernmental organizations, grassroots community organizing, and government offices; and (4) captured mechanisms, the often-unstated emotional reactions activated by the cross-sector collaboration intervention (Ahmed & Ali, 2006; Campbell, Nair, & Maimane, 2007; Manning & Roessler, 2014; Pridmore et al., 2015; Sanchez et al., 2009). Because of the limited developing-country evidence, both the developed-country evidence base and the systematic review were used to establish the previous evidence base and the collaboration principles that undergirded the PAR process.

## 2.5 Collaboration Principles

Rittel and Webber explain how "the analyst's 'world view' is the strongest determining factor in explaining a discrepancy and, therefore, in resolving a wicked problem" (Rittel & Webber, 1973, p. 166). With that said, it is important to understand the "world view" – the collaboration principles – that undergirded this research. At the beginning, these were not clearly articulated ideas but rather areas where a stakeholder-driven approach, informed by the evidence, with data collected based on the stakeholders' decision making, might advance the existing evidence. Some of these principles did not work (and are not discussed in this Element). Those described in Sections 2.5.2–2.5.8 (see Figure 5) became part of the PAR intervention results (see Figure 10).

### 2.5.1 Identifying a Complex Challenge

In their first review of the evidence, Bryson, Crosby, and Stone (2006, p. 45) looked at the factors preceding cross-sector collaboration and explained two ways that organizations go about pursuing it:

> On one hand, our own view is that organizational participants in effective cross-sector collaborations typically have to *fail* into their role in the collaboration. In other words, organizations will only collaborate when they cannot get what they want without collaborating. The second response is to *assume* that collaboration is the Holy Grail of solutions and always best. Often, governments and foundations insist that funding recipients collaborate, even if they have little evidence that it will work. [internal citations omitted]

1. Asking stakeholders to identify something they were not able to do within their own sector will lead to identification of a complex challenge.

2. Through cross-sector collaboration, a facilitator can create a value-neutral understanding of the conflict between the government and the community and work develop a shared understanding. With shared understanding, complex challenges become a series of technical challenges for which the stakeholders can work as a "technical" team to design solutions.

3. "Middle-out" collaboration is necessary when there is a conflicted relationship between government and community stakeholders, and neither is positioned to develop the most effective strategic response to complex challenges.

4. Emergent design and governance — characterized by stakeholders making strategic choices about research methodology, participant selection, context, and projects — will build a strong PAR process.

5. Stakeholders that resource their own participation will have "buy-in," and be more committed to a long-term collaboration process.

6. A process and projects resourced by local stakeholders will build sustainability.

7. Facilitation of consensus through the PAR process provides rigor necessary for collaboration around a complex challenge.

**Figure 5** Collaboration principles

These two characterizations are consistent with the findings from the literature review for this project (Kritz, 2017, 2018). The developed-country evidence now offers a number of ways to assess the need for, and potential efficacy of, a cross-sector collaboration, which is recommended when there is a clear advantage to be gained – for example, when there is sector failure (Bryson, Crosby, & Stone, 2006, 2015). However, in a developing-country setting, where technical sectors are not as strong and indicators can vary widely based on the population, geography, and other factors, it was not clear how to identify sector failure.

In this project, the research director asked the initial stakeholders from multiple sectors, Boateng, Sr. Matilda, and Imoro Toyibu, to identify a challenge that they were not able to address on their own to identify a true complex challenge and sector failure. They identified Old Fadama as the challenge that they wanted to address. However, because urban slums are such a pervasive and growing issue, it was not clear whether any slum would be perceived as sector failure – perhaps these were environments where each sector could point to another that had failed. Or, perhaps slums had replaced rural areas as the "end of the road," areas the government needed to address, to take a next step in providing services, but not necessarily perceived as failures.

However, Old Fadama stood out for one particular reason: multiple times per year, cholera epidemics began in the slum and swept throughout the country. The local government received constant negative local media attention, and more recent epidemics were reported in the international media, worrying high-level government officials that the reports would have a negative effect on tourism and the choice of Ghana as a venue for hosting international meetings. The director of public health documented how similar efforts combatted cholera in other slums but did not work in Old Fadama. He perceived these repeated epidemics as reflecting sector failure.

### 2.5.2 Creating Shared Understanding

Cross-sector collaboration creates shared understanding of complex challenges (Bryson, Crosby, & Stone, 2015), but it is not an easy task to create shared understanding in a high-conflict environment such as Old Fadama. This context requires a conflict-sensitive approach (Anderson, 1999; World Health Organization, 2019). Conflict can be value neutral and is important in that it surfaces issues that need to be addressed for those in conflict to begin to collaborate (Carpenter, 2019). However, these conflicts need to be handled with care to achieve solutions (Bingham, 2009). The PAR interviews were used in part to infuse the process with references to local culture and values regarding the importance of working together, respecting others, and seeking understanding across divisions. The research team used the PAR process to build on these norms and create a shared understanding of Old Fadama's challenges. To do so, the facilitator focused on the stakeholders' shared interests rather than their "positions," by identifying each stakeholder's basic human and organizational needs and focusing attention on doing the best "for Mother Ghana" (see Figure 6). Thus, the PAR process was used to create a value-neutral understanding of the conflict between the government and the community, which provided the opportunity to develop a shared understanding of the challenges.

These norms have further developed and include both a shared terminology and a value system based on mutual respect and understanding (Thomson & Perry, 2006). As the norms grew, new stakeholders were able to more rapidly

**Figure 6** Old Fadama community meeting

expand their perspective, understand the PAR process, share their ideas, and see these ideas incorporated, because of the shared understanding of and language around Old Fadama's challenges.

### 2.5.3 Middle-out Collaboration

In developing countries, cross-sector collaboration often works "top-down" consistent with the flow of development aid funding, or "bottom-up," through work with communities (Kritz, 2017). These processes are anchored in powerful constituencies that help to orient the work. Because of the conflicted relationship between the municipal government and Old Fadama, neither government nor community was positioned to lead the other. An organization was needed to bridge this divide, and the research director created the term "middle-out collaboration" to define this leadership role.

If government does not mandate cross-sector collaboration, the literature suggests starting with a small group of stakeholders and expanding the collaboration as the momentum grows (Bryson, Crosby, & Stone, 2015). This approach requires strategic relationship building (Magrab & Raper, 2010). The research director designed the middle-out stakeholder identification to determine those organizations best positioned to bridge the divide around Old Fadama. Catholic sisters – because of their moral leadership, demonstrated capacity to work with communities and reputation for long-term commitment to fill gaps in government social service delivery – were enrolled as research participants to sit in the "middle" and build a bridge "out" between government and the community.

### 2.5.4 Emergent Design and Governance

The collaboration literature describes a range of design and governance possibilities from formal structures to informal interactions through which decisions can be made (Bryson, Crosby, & Stone, 2006; Provan & Milward, 1995; Stone, Crosby, & Bryson, 2013). Employing deliberate, formal design and governance in the context of already planned interventions is consistent with the literature on developing-country collaborative projects (Kritz, 2017). By contrast, emergent design allows missions, goals, roles, and action steps to emerge over time within a network of involved or affected parties to overcome problems in a system (Bryson, Crosby, & Stone, 2015).

Leading journals identify a significant research gap around public participation in developing countries. When the gap is viewed from the field of psychology, it is clear that this sort of participation requires both processes and readiness of those whose participation is sought (Moghaddam, 2016). Ideally, a citizen must be guided by a critical and open mind, while government must accept and respond to appropriate criticism. Emergent design addressed both the readiness of the governing (city government and slum leadership) and the governed (slum leadership and residents) to participate in a more transparent process that evolved to meet their needs at the same time (Kritz & Moghaddam, 2018).

Because Old Fadama was an informal settlement that developed on land set aside as an eco-zone or preserve, government infrastructure planning did not include that geographic area. Civil servants were unable to take up the challenge of infrastructure planning for a variety of reasons. For example, the government created its budgets around city planning maps that did not include the settlement, so creating a budget for slum improvement would require changing the city plan. More immediately, solid waste pickup or installing water pipes and sanitation required creating road access, which would displace residents with nowhere else to go.

More recent scholarship explains how informal norms of settlement and belonging – specifically the interaction between indigenous landowners and migrants – structure everyday politics and spill over into formal elections (Paller, 2019). Because the slum contained a large population of voters with ties throughout the country, politicians were wary about angering the community. Politicians had historically made promises about slum upgrading, but these promises had not been kept. Slum leadership resorted to leveraging media attention to demand dialogue with the government and advocate for better infrastructure, but this only created more tension and led to at least one failed infrastructure project.

Conflict is value neutral; if managed productively, it can be used as an opportunity to galvanize stakeholders to try different solutions (Carpenter, 2019). However, learning to use conflict productively takes time. Emergent design and governance, where stakeholders make strategic choices about research methodology, participants, context, and projects allowed stakeholders time to learn to work through their conflicts, thus building a strong PAR process.

### 2.5.5 Creating "Buy-In"

The evidence from psychology suggested that stakeholders' investment in various projects would increase their likelihood of continuing to participate, thus strengthening their bonds to the projects (Festinger, 1962). Thus, to increase stakeholder commitment or buy-in, the collaboration principle was that the stakeholders must find the necessary human and physical resources for their own participation and projects. Previously, the stakeholders were accustomed to development projects, funded by northern governments and international donor organizations, that supported all local participation and project costs. The idea of resourcing their own participation and projects challenged their thinking in a positive way. Early in this project, consistent with old expectations the international development projects created, stakeholders made numerous requests for payments and asked for laptops, smart phones, and other tools. Over time, however, these requests diminished. As the facilitator introduced the project to new stakeholders, he explained that the project was a "public good" being done "for Mother Ghana," so "we all should put in our own resources." As new stakeholders "bought in" to this shared vision, they did so with the understanding that they would be developing projects based on the resources at their disposal or that they raised together.

### 2.5.6 Building for Sustainability

A growing body of research offers perspective on process-oriented studies such as this one (Brownson, Colditz, & Proctor, 2012; Peters et al., 2013; Spiegelman, 2016). However, implementation of sustainable projects in developing countries has proven to be challenging, despite the focus on this concept (Gruen et al., 2008; Shediac-Rizkallah & Bone, 1998). A frequently documented challenge is that when northern international development funding ends, the projects stop working, thus erasing the supposed gains from the effort. One factor of this issue is that the international development funding drove the project. Stakeholders resourcing of their own participation through all phases of a project is one key to sustainability (Fowler, 2001). For this PAR project, the principle was that if the stakeholders resourced their own participation, the process would be created with local funds, building toward sustainability.

### 2.5.7 Requiring Consensus

Collaborative governance is an explicit strategy for incorporating stakeholders into government policy and planning through "multilateral and consensus-oriented decision processes" (Ansell & Gash, 2008, p. 548). Collaboration requires a commitment to process that goes beyond the initial design (Bryson et al., 2011a; Mintzberg, Ahlstrand, & Lampel, 1998). The research director trained the local facilitator on the collaboration evidence and together they began to develop the PAR process. The evidence suggests that these kinds of "bridging social capital" roles are one important facet of development (Carpenter, 2019; Woolcock & Narayan, 2000). The research director, facilitator, and community liaison (the research team) collected all data and engaged the stakeholders through interviews, focus groups, a survey, and continuous data collection and triangulation. Throughout the PAR process, the research team used the cross-sector collaboration evidence base as a guide, to support the PAR process, educate the stakeholders, and inform their decision making. The principle was that a consensus-based PAR process would provide a level of rigor suitable for collaboration around a complex challenge.

### 2.5.8 Application of the Collaboration Principles

The research director introduced the concept of cross-sector collaboration at the outset of the project. The research team educated the stakeholders about the developed- and developing-country evidence base; supported the stakeholders through PAR in forming a cross-sector collaboration; and developed priorities, strategies, and projects with the stakeholders. This process generated the data that the research team collected, analyzed, and shared with the stakeholders so that they could understand their own decision making. Utilizing grounded theory helped to make sense of the data and to develop a theoretical account of the process. The social sciences employ grounded theory as an "inductive, theory discovery methodology that allows a researcher to develop a theoretical account of the general features of a topic while simultaneously, grounding the account in empirical observations or data" (Martin & Turner, 1986, p. 141). Section 3 describes how the PAR process unfolded, and the role of these collaboration principles in expanding the process.

## 3 The Accra Stakeholder Platform: Designing a Cross-sector Collaboration Intervention

Rapid urban migration, leading to the growth of urban slums, is a worldwide phenomenon. Africa has been urbanizing at a rate of 3.5 percent per year during the past two decades, a rate that is expected to continue until 2050 (African Development Bank Group, 2012). In Ghana, migration to urban areas coupled with a severe housing shortage has given rise to rapidly growing slums (Paller, 2015). Hundreds of thousands of people have flooded the cities seeking liberation from increasingly difficult lives. As of 2014, an estimated 37.9 percent of Ghana's urban dwellers (United Nations Statistics Division, Department of Economic and Social Affairs, 2014a) or 5,349,300 people lived in slums (United Nations Statistics Division, Department of Economic and Social Affairs, 2014b).

The United Nations Human Settlement Program defines slums by physical conditions including lack of durable and permanent housing, sufficient living space, access to safe water and sanitation, and security of tenure that prevents forced evictions (United Nations Human Settlement Program, 2006). These conditions contribute to a multitude of development challenges, including high rates of environmental deterioration, poverty, and unemployment; high levels of conflict and gender-based violence; overcrowding; and poor sanitation and waste management. These complex challenges impact all sectors and often result in protracted and entrenched conflicts.

The research director's initial goal for this project was to develop an evidence-based, stakeholder-driven PAR intervention to create cross-sector collaboration.[1] This meant that the research needed to incorporate analysis of the PAR process, as well as the way that any projects shaped it. Additional goals that were developed through the PAR process, with the facilitator, community liaison, and stakeholders, were that the collaboration should work to resolve complex challenges in Old Fadama and that the PAR process had the potential to be scaled up sustainably. See Figure 7 for definitions of this terminology.

Section 3.1 describes the research director's exploratory research to identify initial stakeholders and a slum community. Section 3.2 begins with a discussion of PAR as a tool to create and strategically manage cross-sector collaboration. The research team used the PAR process to introduce the concept of cross-sector collaboration, educate the stakeholders about the existing evidence, and support them in forming a cross-sector collaboration. The research methods and

---

[1] Study participants provided informed consent before taking part in the research. The Social Science and Behavioral Institutional Review Board at Georgetown University (Protocol No. 2015–0261 MOD00004778, CR00002280) and Ghana Health Service Ethical Review Committee (Protocol No. GHS-ERC 10/03/15) granted research approval.

1. Evidence-based means that, throughout the process, the stakeholders were informed of the developed- and developing-country evidence, were given an opportunity to reflect on the options presented by the evidence base and the situation they were evaluating, and made decisions that they understood were consistent with the evidence base or departed from the evidence base.

2. Stakeholders are those who are engaged in cross-sector collaboration, providing time or resources to resolve a challenge. The Old Fadama stakeholders call their form of organization their "collaboration" or "stakeholder platform." Research participants are stakeholders who participated in formal data collection; some stakeholders did not participate in formal data collection, usually because the research team felt the process reached saturation.

3. Stakeholder-driven means that the stakeholders selected the location and focus of the study and made all strategy and project decisions including stakeholders to involve, projects to undertake, and when to move to the next stage of the process. When this Element describes how the stakeholders or "the collaboration" took an action, that means that all research participants — who make up the collaboration — reached consensus on that course of action and those taking the action were considered to be doing so on behalf of "the collaboration."

4. Intervention means a package of collaboration principles and a PAR process to build cross-sector collaboration. The intervention was designed without a focus on one sector so the stakeholders could identify new challenges and create new strategies and projects to resolve them.

5. Analysis at the process management level means that data was collected in order to feed back into and strategically manage the collaboration. Evaluation at the project level means that projects needed to be analyzed as to their impact on the collaboration.

6. The facilitator, Mr. Peter N. Batsa was engaged to collect data and serve as the collaboration's facilitator. His organization, National Catholic Health Service, was a research organization that brought significant planning and research skills to the process. They served as a bridging organization (Carpenter, 2019; Manning & Roessler, 2014), needed because of the conflicted relationship between the municipal government and the community. The facilitation literature describes this vital role as creating consultative meetings and platforms for discussion to build relationships and accountability between differently resourced organizations with different capacities (Kritz, 2017).

7. The community liaison, Sr. Rita Ann Kusi, HDR, of the Handmaids of the Divine Redeemer congregation of Catholic sisters, was engaged to collect data and serve as the collaboration's community liaison. Her congregation served as a bridging organization (Carpenter, 2019; Manning & Roessler, 2014), needed because of the conflicted relationship between the municipal government and the community.

8. Resolved means that the stakeholders wanted to resolve challenges at the strategic level or root cause. "Social problems are never solved" (Rittel & Webber, 1973), so stakeholders' programmatic solutions were developed based on strategy that they considered would lead to sustainability.

9. Complex challenges or adaptive challenges are largely social, affecting many different people, systems and sectors and generally defined through finding a solution to the problem itself (Rittel & Webber, 1973).

10. The Old Fadama community of Accra was the focus of this research study. In Phase I, the community was represented by a community member who worked for the municipal government. In Phase II, three community chiefs joined as research participants in the study. In Phase III, a community survey was used to engage a broader range of community members. Later in the process, all chiefs were involved in planning latrine installation.

11. Scale-up is the stakeholder-driven and locally resourced process of expanding the project according to the stakeholder needs and interests. Additional terms include adoption and replication, which are different methods of expanding a project.

12. Sustainable, for this project, is defined as when organizations refine their operations to incorporate cross-sector collaboration into their practices, projects address the root cause of the complex challenges the stakeholders choose to address, and human resources and project costs are resourced locally.

**Figure 7** Definitions

development of the PAR phases are described in detail, including interviews, focus group discussions (FGD), and a community survey. Section 3.3 explains the piloting and results of the intervention components.

## 3.1 Exploratory Research to Identify Stakeholders and Community

This section explains in further detail the initial stakeholder identification described in Section 1. The research director began by identifying, in a purposive process, possible research participants who could work together to identify a challenge. Catholic sisters seemed to be the nongovernmental actors best-known in Ghana for making consistent, long-term commitments to poor and marginalized communities. The National Catholic Health Service identified a purposive sample of four sisters from congregations known for their work with the poor, who might want to participate. Congregations are religious organizations of sisters dedicated to social service in the world, rather than a monastic or cloistered way of life. There has been a concerted push in international development to engage faith organizations (Duff & Buckingham, 2015). However, they are nearly absent from the collaboration literature, so it was unclear if the sisters would enroll (Kritz, 2017). The research director interviewed them, and Sr. Matilda Sorkpor, HDR (the "lead sister") agreed to participate and chose Old Fadama as a place she wanted to work but was hesitant to enter because the challenge was so great. In 2018–2019, she educated and enrolled several additional sisters from different congregations.

The municipal government seemed to be a logical partner because Old Fadama was an urban slum. When the research director contacted Boateng, the director of public health of the Accra Metropolitan Assembly (the AMA, the mayor's office), he responded with enthusiasm and relief:

> Thank God you are here. We need help. Everything we have tried in this community seems to fail. I am meeting with the press again this morning about the cholera epidemic that originated there. We can't find the solution to this problem on our own. I am willing to try anything.

Little is documented about effective government partnership in the scholarly literature, so it was unclear what to expect from government participation (Barnes, Brown, & Harman, 2016). Through interviews, representatives of the Department of Public Health shared that their typical efforts combatted cholera in other areas but did not work in Old Fadama. The evidence suggests that sectoral failure is an antecedent to cross-sector collaboration, and a facilitating organization can assist collaboration formation (Bryson, Crosby, & Stone, 2006). Consistent with that evidence, and because of the research focus and Catholic sisters' engagement, Boateng and others from the Department of Public Health became enthusiastic partners. They supported community involvement and provided public and environmental health research to inform stakeholders' decision making. Later, when the research participants undertook a latrine project, the Department of Public Health coordinated between AMA offices that scoped the latrines, developed plans, and provided resources for permits, beginning to change the city's policy around Old Fadama slum improvement.

**Figure 8** Old Fadama community elder

As described in Section 1, the Old Fadama community was represented by Imoro Toyibu, a resident who had served for years as its secretary and has recently been hired as the municipal government's public health officer for Old Fadama. After the initial interviews, he identified several research participants, leaders from Old Fadama community organizations. These included the Kayayei Youth Association, a community association of women and girls locally known as "kayayei," head porters who carry goods (typically balanced on their heads) in markets and sell products on the streets throughout Accra; and the Old Fadama Youth Development Association (OFADA), the Old Fadama community association governed by the chiefs (community elders, see Figure 8) of the sixteen tribes residing in Old Fadama. OFADA did not include the chiefs of the two warring tribes that many believed were responsible for much of the organized violence in the slum. However, the association represented the majority of Old Fadama residents. Those familiar with community-based approaches know that the idea of a community may "create the illusion that people in a particular location, neighborhood, or ethnic group, are necessarily cooperative, caring, and inclusive. The reality may be very different, as power differentials in gender, race, and class relations may result in exclusion, and threaten the apparent cohesiveness of the group in question" (Mathie & Cunningham, 2003, p. 475). Consistent with the evidence, Old Fadama was not homogeneous, and decision making and negotiation often took place along tribal lines (Paller, 2014). A number of other community leaders and members also enrolled as research participants to offer their input on strategy and projects.

Two National Catholic Health Service (NCHS) officers served as the Ghana-based facilitation and research team. NCHS is a local organization, an association of Catholic health institutions that provides research and planning services and coordinates with government health services. The director of NCHS provided early guidance on collaboration with sisters and identified a staff member, Peter Batsa, to collect data and serve as the collaboration's facilitator. The facilitation literature describes this vital role as creating consultative meetings and platforms for discussion to build relationships and accountability between differently resourced organizations with different capacities (Kritz, 2017). A number of case studies in the literature detail important facilitation skills and responsibilities. These include research (Campbell, Nair, & Maimane, 2007; Pridmore et al., 2015; Sanchez et al., 2005), as well as catalyzing (Saadé, Bateman, & Bendahmane, 2001), linking (Kielmann et al., 2014), bridging (Manning & Roessler, 2014), brokering (Sablah et al., 2012) or serving as an intermediary (Murthy et al., 2001; Probandari et al., 2011), coordinating (Brooke-Sumner, Lund, & Petersen, 2016; Thaennin, Visuthismajarn, & Sutheravut, 2012), convening (Li et al., 2015), and facilitating (Manning & Roessler, 2014; Rangan et al., 2004; Wessells, 2015).

Due to the complexity of Old Fadama's problems, all of these responsibilities were deemed essential. As the collaboration grew, a Catholic sister, Sr. Rita Ann Kusi, HDR, joined the research team to serve in the important role of community liaison. The data later showed that her presence conveyed the message that this was a nonpolitical, public interest effort, thus building trust in the community and differentiating this project from efforts to sway voters in the lead-up to the contentious 2016 national elections. Later in the project, she received a grant to build a block of latrines in partnership with the municipal government and with input from the Old Fadama community.

Each research participant informed and sought input from their own important constituencies – stakeholders within their own organizations as well as others. As examples, Boateng consulted the leadership of the Ga State, a politically powerful Accra group with a historic ownership interest in the Old Fadama land. NCHS and the sisters consulted the Ghana Catholic Bishops Conference and the Office of the Metropolitan Archbishop. These offices represent the hierarchy of the Catholic Church and supported the sisters' work in a coordinated manner. In time, some constituents became stakeholders. For example, as the project progressed, Boateng liaised with the Ministry of Inner-City and Zongo Development and the Ghana Health Service, government ministries that offered their input and later became stakeholders when the community and municipal priorities aligned with their offices' national planning goals. Figure 9 describes the

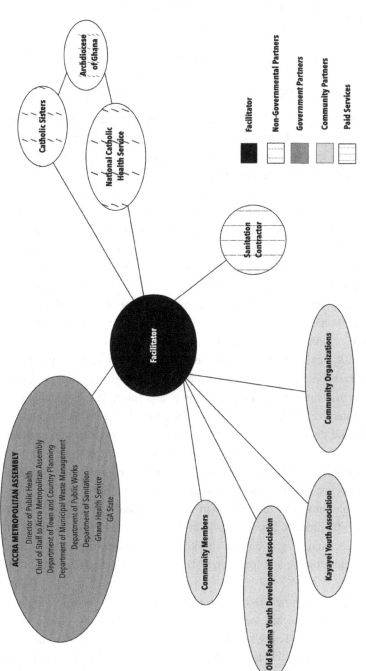

**Figure 9** Stakeholder diagram

research participants and their stakeholders (Ministry of Health, Archdiocese of Ghana, Ga State) who joined the collaboration between 2015, when it began, and 2017, the end of the concept phase.

## 3.2 Development of the Participatory Action Research (PAR) Intervention Components: Interviews, Focus Group Discussions (FGD), and a Community Survey

As described, the stakeholders began by identifying a challenge that they would like to try to address through cross-sector collaboration, using their own resources and applying for funding as needed. There were three PAR phases: (1) key informant interviews with Catholic sisters identified a location for the study, to which the municipal Department of Public Health agreed; (2) focus group discussions (FGDs) set community priorities, aligned them with the priorities of government planning, and created strategies and projects; and (3) a community survey increased community member participation and further defined project goals and measurement.

Participatory action research couples knowledge generation – such as would occur in traditional research – with an additional component: a process to create or support organizational action and change (Cornwall & Jewkes, 1995; Greenwood & Levin, 1998). PAR was identified as a methodology that could meet the stakeholders' needs in a complex environment, including a rapidly evolving urban slum, a diffuse city agency, and multiple congregations of Catholic sisters that were taught to plan strategically and work together as they made the decision to move from better-served rural areas to an urban slum. PAR incorporates local priorities, processes, and perspectives (Cornwall & Jewkes, 1995). A PAR process involves researchers and participants working together to define the problem and formulate context-specific research questions and solutions. The research team and participants worked together to create the PAR process. They made joint decisions to establish the research agenda; collect and analyze data on stakeholders' opinions; identify priorities, strategies, and projects; and incorporate the resulting knowledge into the PAR process.

These steps transformed each participating organizations' practices in comparison with the way they worked in the past, and the way other similar organizations worked. The research team incorporated a holistic understanding of the context of each of the stakeholder organizations, including their structures and history with cross-sector collaboration, cultures, organizational norms, and strategies. Through the use of qualitative methods, the research team was able to understand the stakeholders' organizations' practices within their own contexts, why cross-sector collaboration was the tool they chose to employ, and where evidence could inform their decision making (Cornwall & Jewkes, 1995; Miles, Huberman, & Saldana, 2014).

Throughout the process, the research team used purposive sampling to select research participants based on their perspective and role (Stringer, 1999), and intensity sampling based on the understanding of current information and the need to fill remaining gaps (Patton, 2015). The research team took participant observation notes at all interviews and focus groups, as well as during the survey and meetings. Most focus groups were audio recorded. The focus groups allowed the research team to observe stakeholder interactions within the context of their own organization and between organizations. As noted in the Figure 7, the terms "research participants" and "participants" are used to describe those who formally participated in data collection to inform the study. The term "stakeholders" is used to describe groups including participants as well as others who did not participate in formal data collection, usually because the process was believed to have achieved saturation. The methodology of the project included continuous data collection, and the research team remained nimble, faced with constantly shifting contextual dynamics that are common in an unstable, rapidly developing urban slum. Consistent with the evidence base, as a result, the process was reflexive, flexible, and iterative (Cornwall & Jewkes, 1995). Ghana is an Anglophone country, so the process was conducted in English except where otherwise noted.

## 3.3 Piloting and Results of the Intervention Components

The research director suggested initial steps, with significant input by Sr. Matilda and the Department of Public Health. Reflecting PAR principles developed around priority setting, throughout the process the research team trained the stakeholders on the relevant collaboration evidence, supported their decision making, and collected data from the stakeholders to feed back into the process (Patten, Mitton, & Donaldson, 2006). Each phase resulted in decision making by consensus, meaning that all stakeholders came to agreement on the decision. Thus, when this Element describes how "the collaboration" took an action, that means research participants in a full FGD or smaller FGD reached a consensus-based decision, decided on a follow-up action, and designated one or more research participants to take that action on behalf of all participants in the collaboration. The results of each PAR phase are organized by the two main themes that emerged: process management of the cross-sector collaboration and strategy and project development based on the stakeholders' priorities. There were three phases to the PAR process.

### 3.3.1 Phase I: Key Informant Interviews and Process Management Results

In February 2015, as described in Section 3.1, the research director conducted in-depth, semi-structured interviews that lasted between one and four hours, with a purposive sample of eleven potential stakeholders: five non-governmental (four congregations of Catholic sisters and NCHS), six governmental (three AMA and three Ghana Health Service), and one community member. The scholarly literature suggested interview themes including experience with collaboration, strategic interests of each individual and their organizations, and prior relationships among the interviewees (Kritz, 2017). The interview protocol was later adapted (Appendix A) for use in initial interviews with new stakeholders. Interviews were recorded through note-taking, along with detailed notes on emerging issues, ideas, activities, and informal conversations with key actors. This practice enhanced reflexivity, supported active listening in the interview process, and enabled triangulation with other data during the analysis stage. The research director constructed the interviews to educate the interviewees about cross-sector collaboration.

Through the interviews, the three initial stakeholders described earlier agreed to enroll as research participants. The research director triangulated the interview data with follow-up email and telephone conversations for clarification and used qualitative content analysis to identify themes, areas of consensus, important strategies to explore, cultural norms around the idea of working together, as well as terminology, common expressions, and key concepts related to cross-sector collaboration in Ghana. Two themes emerged: (1) due to the volatile nature of the slum environment, process management of the collaboration required significant attention and (2) projects were needed to address community needs, which included understanding community priorities along with prior strategies and efforts to address them.

All interviewees were unfamiliar with the term "cross-sector collaboration." When it was described to them, 100 percent said they worked through cross-sector collaboration in the past. Each of the stakeholders understood cross-sector collaboration as a method through which they naturally operated in some cases. They all understood that it is a very challenging approach and appreciated that it is valued as highly effective when it succeeds. Agreed-upon local terminology, common expressions, and key concepts resulting from the interviews were used and refined throughout the process.

The research participants reached consensus on several process results. The first was a decision to focus on the Old Fadama slum because it presented perhaps the greatest challenge to Accra's development. This decision shaped Collaboration Principle 1, identification of a complex challenge. The second result was the stakeholders' willingness to participate in cross-sector collaboration to solve problems with this community. This decision, along with an agreement to resource their own participation, became Collaboration Principle 5. The third result was consensus on the importance of engaging Old Fadama community leaders to design and implement a strategy, coupled with agreement on the importance of not contacting them until the stakeholders were ready to take action so as to not "disappoint" the leaders. This decision shaped Collaboration Principle 4, to employ emergent design and governance.

In June 2015, heavy rains caused floodwaters to rise to the tops of Old Fadama buildings. Flooding throughout the city killed or injured more than three hundred people. Many Accra residents believed the slum caused the flooding. They blamed the residents specifically for infilling and silting the river and lagoon. As a result, the AMA demolished the area of Old Fadama that encroached upon the river and lagoon. They provided transport for displaced residents, even paying some of them to return to their homes in northern Ghana. The resettlement effort was ineffective: many residents jumped from the transport before even leaving Accra, while others used the transport as an opportunity for a free ride to visit home, returning to Accra later in the year. The bulldozing and resettlement caused considerable tension that erupted into violence. These developments also demonstrated that bridge building between the municipal government and the community was absolutely essential, leading to the idea of middle-out collaboration that became Collaboration Principle 3. This project's three initial research participants considered changing locations due to the increased violence and anger. However, they decided to continue to work in Old Fadama because, after the flooding and the failed resettlement, the residents' need was even greater.

### 3.3.2 Phase II: Focus Group Discussions (FGDs)

As noted in Section 2.5.3, when cross-sector collaboration is not government mandated, the literature suggests starting with a small group of stakeholders and expanding as the momentum grows (Bryson, Crosby, & Stone, 2015). Citizen participation in government planning is known to be increasingly important (Fagence, 2014). However, there is a gap in research around participation in government planning in Africa (Kapiriri, Ole Frithjof, & Kristian, 2003; Maluka, 2011). The PAR process was designed to build government capacity to incorporate citizen participation, so that data from the grassroots could inform government planning.

The research director and initial stakeholders agreed that the next step should be a meeting to involve community leadership. As described earlier, due to the conflicted relationship between the municipal government and the community, it was clear that neither could facilitate the collaboration due to a lack of trust. It was at this point that Batsa was engaged as a facilitator to collect data on the PAR process and to work alongside the Catholic sisters and build bridges between these conflicted parties. In all, there were four FGDs, designed to engage the community leadership, identify community priorities, align these priorities with government planning, create strategies, and implement a project. The research director and the facilitator designed the FGDs and collected the data, audio recording the focus groups for later analysis. Participant observation was important, so interactions were captured through note-taking, including recording nonverbal expressions.

Batsa facilitated each FGD. He and the research director provided consultation on cross-sector collaboration theory and evidence to inform the research participants. During each FGD, the facilitator worked with existing research participants to identify new stakeholders, based on the criterion that they might play a long-term role in implementing the project strategy. Research participants achieved consensus on identifying additional participants to invite. Based on prior experiences with short-term interventions, the research participants' criteria excluded international NGOs, which are generally funded for short project cycles that are unsuitable for complex challenges such as Old Fadama.

The research director and facilitator constructed the FGDs (Appendix B) to give all participants the opportunity to express their own thoughts about the collaboration process and projects. The research director used qualitative content analysis to understand participants' shared opinions on process management, priorities, strategies, and projects. The research director triangulated the results from each FGD with the participants, facilitator, and initial stakeholders (Boateng, Imoro, and Sr. Matilda). Because the results captured decisions that were made by consensus, triangulating usually meant ensuring the language of the results matched the stakeholders' intention and confirming their agreement (given a chance to think more about it) with the decisions they made. This cross-checking was conducted with the initial stakeholders and other participants in each FGD, until the research team believed consensus was achieved. In this way, the results were continuously updated based on developments in the community and among the stakeholders. The research team analyzed the data for each FGD separately and then together as a whole to understand differences in the FGD participants' attitudes, beliefs, and opinions and how these changed over time. These results, too, were shared with the initial stakeholders and the participants in each FGD in an iterative way to continually update the research participants on the decision making.

### FGD 1: Catholic Sisters (Eight Catholic Sisters, Purposive Sample)

The sisters' FGD was conducted in Sr. Matilda's offices with eight participants from three Catholic sisters' congregations focused on community work. This FGD was interesting in that the participating congregations freely gave feedback on the Old Fadama collaboration, but other than Sr. Matilda's congregation, they were not interested in joining as research participants. It was not clear why, at the time. However, the research director later learned from members of the Catholic Church hierarchy that there had been a history of serious collaboration failure and resulting conflict between sisters' congregations in Accra. Neither the sisters participating in the FGD nor in fact any of the sisters currently working in Accra participated in the collaboration failure or were even aware of it. However, the failure was thought to have shaped their organizational norms. As a result, the church hierarchy perceived collaboration between sisters' congregations in Accra as very challenging.

**Results: Process Management.** All Catholic sisters had prior experience with cross-sector collaboration. They recognized, as a priority, becoming better able to represent their congregations in collaborations and develop associated skills. They believed it was very important to work with community leaders to "do what the community wants" in the development of community activities. They agreed to investigate whether it was politically feasible to work in Old Fadama, in light of their existing organizational relationships.

**Results: Strategies and Projects.** Catholic sisters in Ghana are generally focused on rural areas. The sisters expressed the importance of working in Old Fadama, although they had little experience working in urban areas. They agreed to identify sisters or other Catholic Church projects in Old Fadama and the urban slums of Accra, to see if there were projects they might join or replicate.

### FGD 2: Full Stakeholders (Purposive Sample: Seven AMA, Two Catholic Sisters, Six Community)

The second FGD, in July 2015, was a full stakeholders meeting held one month after the AMA's partial demolition of the slum. Fifteen stakeholders met, including seven from government (AMA – including Boateng and Toyibu), two nongovernmental (including Sr. Matilda), and six from the Old Fadama community (including two leaders of community organizations and three community chiefs, one of whom was an imam). It was the first meeting to include the community leadership, and the meeting was fraught with tension because of the demolition and the resulting homelessness for tens of thousands of slum residents. The leaders of the community organizations, who were not Ghanaian and did not live in Old Fadama but worked there daily, angrily criticized Boateng, the director of public health, for the demolition. It was clear to all that he was not consulted about the demolition in advance. Rather than debate the demolition, Boateng maintained his focus on his excitement that this was the first-ever meeting between community leaders and the AMA Department of Public Health in the department's offices. At the end of the meeting, the community chiefs pulled the research director aside and said apologetically that the international representatives who criticized Boateng were "not Ghanaian – not behaving in a Ghanaian way, and they do not represent us." The chiefs confirmed that they were grateful for the opportunity to collaborate and would do their best to work with the Department of Public Health.

**Results: Process Management.** Participants expressed a concept encountered earlier, that they were unfamiliar with the term "cross-sector collaboration" but had prior experience with it in practice. They agreed that cross-sector collaboration would be useful in solving Old Fadama's problems and expressed willingness to participate. They recognized that each organization represented at the meeting could play a unique role in responding to challenges in Old Fadama. Themes that had consensus were the value of working together as a team, the AMA's knowledge of community problems, the Department of Public Health's history of working with the community (although the interventions were deemed unsuccessful, the attempts were positively regarded), the Catholic sisters' leadership in social development work with communities, the importance of community leadership, and recognition of the leadership that citizens could offer and the obligation that citizens have to take part in community development.

**Results: Strategies and Projects.** Priorities discussed in detail included sanitation, solid waste collection, vulnerable kayayei (head porter) women and girls and particularly gender-based violence against them, and access to clean water. There was consensus that water delivery was the most politically feasible project, especially if it focused on children. The community requested sanitation in prior meetings with the mayor; although this option was agreed to be the highest priority because, as one community chief said, "cholera is killing us today," it was also agreed to be the least feasible for political and logistical reasons. The research team agreed to develop white papers on each priority. This meeting demonstrated the importance of a skilled facilitator, who could build relationships between the stakeholders while implementing the PAR process, leading to Collaboration Principle 7.

### FGD 3: Initial Stakeholders (Purposive Sample: Senior Representatives)

The third FGD was conducted in September 2015 at Georgetown University, in Washington, DC, alongside an international conference on migration. Because of the factionalism in community politics – as described earlier, decision making and negotiation often took place along tribal lines (Paller, 2014) – the community leadership was not able to participate because that would have necessitated inviting all sixteen leaders to fly to Washington, DC, which was cost prohibitive. The meeting included the senior representatives of the initial stakeholders (Boateng from the AMA Department of Public Health and Sr. Matilda, the lead sister) and George Adjei, director of the National Catholic Health Service (NCHS), the facilitating organization.

**Results: Process Management.** This FGD was constructed as a smaller group to build stakeholders' relationships, educate them about the latest research on migration issues so that they could better understand Old Fadama, present their cross-sector collaboration as a solution, and practice discussing their work publicly.

**Results: Strategies and Projects.** There was consensus that water, sanitation, and solid waste collection were still the priorities. Participants tested multiple strategies and implementation scenarios and agreed upon roles and responsibilities. They agreed that the water delivery project discussed in FGD2 would be most feasible but not sustainable; therefore, they decided not to pursue that project. Consistent with FGD2, sanitation was the top priority. Because of political sensitivities around permanent installation and the potential of another AMA demolition, the participants reached consensus on a project to install portable latrines.

By the time the director of public health returned home to Accra after the meeting, he had changed his perspective. He said he realized that of all the presenters at the international migration conference, he was the sole government representative working with a slum community. Numerous other presentations at the conference detailed government missteps, bad actions, and negative consequences for slum populations. The director of public health believed that cross-sector collaboration was a cutting-edge solution, and that Accra and Ghana could be important leaders in rigorous research and modeling around slum upgrading. He decided that despite the political sensitivities, he would seek to install permanent latrines in the community to "care for the residents while they are there." Upon returning to Accra, he immediately went to the home of the coordinating director, the AMA's senior civil servant with twenty years' tenure in the office, to brief him on the project, and he received permission to engage other AMA technical offices in permanent latrine installation.

### FGD 4: Technical Planning (Purposive Sample: Five AMA, Sr. Matilda)

The fourth FGD was a technical planning meeting to engage the other AMA technical offices: Public Health, Public Works, and Waste Management. Boateng's goal was to engage them to begin construction on a structure that included a twelve-seat latrine block and a bathhouse with six showers. For ease of reference, this structure is referred to as a "latrine," but the planning was modified with community input to include different bathhouse options as well as a clothes-washing station. The meeting was conducted in the Department of Public Health's offices, with Sr. Matilda and five AMA representatives from the three departments.

**Results: Process Management.** Discussion centered on negotiation between the AMA offices on division of labor around latrine installation. Because of political sensitivities and the need to realign budgets to incorporate this new project, there was consensus that the offices would seek high-level political support before AMA employees took action. There was appreciation that cross-sector collaboration offered the Department of Public Health the opportunity to work in a more coordinated way with other sectors within the AMA, as well as with the chiefs of the sixteen Old Fadama tribes.

**Results: Strategies and Projects.** To plan latrine installation, the city needed to reallocate human resources and budgets. To overcome some of the challenges, Sr. Matilda agreed to supervise construction and management of the latrines. The AMA representatives committed to seeking political support to resource the project, which included drafting plans, ensuring environmental compliance, and paying for and managing the permit process.

### *3.3.3 Phase III: Stakeholder and Community Survey*

The technical planning FGD results were cross-checked with the community leaders from FGD 2, who had been unable, for logistical reasons with transportation, to participate as planned. Having requested latrine installation from the AMA in prior years without success, the community leaders were very enthusiastic about moving forward. They requested a community survey to expand the number of stakeholders and engage community members on latrine construction. This perspective is consistent with the evidence on working with underserved communities (Wallerstein & Duran, 2010). The leaders wanted community member input on two focus areas: (1) latrine management to address maintenance, sustainability, and how the proceeds would be reinvested and (2) site selection with a needs assessment including factors such as migration, population density and movement, and the requirement of moving dwellings to create access for waste removal trucks. At this point, as described in Section 3, a Catholic sister, Sr. Rita Ann Kusi, HDR, joined the research team to serve in the important role of community liaison and to conduct the community interviews.

The research director's goal for the survey (Appendix C) was to understand community needs and interests and explore ideas about cross-sector collaboration and participation. The research director constructed the interview guide to explain the process of cross-sector collaboration and the Catholic sisters' role in installing and managing latrines in the Old Fadama community. The survey explored the relationship among the community members, community leaders, and the AMA. The research team used the survey to identify areas of consensus on the sanitation strategy so that the community, city, and sisters could move forward together. This was a chance, as described earlier, to inform the PAR process of the community's ideas and concurrently create research results that would be useful for government planning.

For each of the two survey themes, collaboration process management and sanitation strategy, there were multiple statements on the questionnaire. There were specific questions about the residents' perceptions on collaboration, as well as the latrine project. The questionnaire employed a Likert scale to measure opinions, followed by open-ended questions to further understand important details. The survey was pretested with sanitation and public health experts from Accra (in and outside Old Fadama) and the United States. The Department of Public Health's officer-in-charge, Imoro Toyibu, who lived in Old Fadama and spoke the residents' local languages, translated the interviews when necessary.

Conducting the survey was challenging for a variety of reasons. One complicating factor was that the latrine business was small and tightly controlled by a few community leaders. The practice was for latrine business owners to generally agree with one another upon a price for latrine usage, with a cost structure based on toilet paper, known as "t-roll," usage: business owners charged the lowest price to provide nothing at all, a higher price for newspaper, and the highest price for t-roll. However, the pricing system broke down when a business owner was in need of extra money. Then, they would frequently and unilaterally raise their prices. Because of Old Fadama's space limitations and indirect pathways, it was often challenging for customers to visit latrines in other areas, so they would either pay these higher prices or be forced to engage in public urination and defecation. The AMA's June 2015 partial demolition destroyed a number of latrines, creating a gap in service. Thus, business owners raised their prices such that many slum residents were not able to access latrines, resulting in increased public defecation and urination.

The second challenge was that the AMA Department of Public Health had already failed in attempts to work with community leaders to install latrines. This negotiation unfolded in an interesting way. While the AMA owned the land in Old Fadama, it was subdivided so that each tribe had the right to use a particular area. Based on cultural custom from northern Ghana, the chiefs decided how to use their tribe's allocated land. In the past, when the AMA attempted to locate a site for the latrine installation, a number of chiefs exercised their ownership interests for the site and the access. By the end of the negotiation, the project cost was more than doubled, which was both outside the AMA budget and not justifiable for ethical reasons. Thus, the AMA's negotiation ended without latrines being installed.

The third and most daunting challenge was that the upcoming elections cast slum improvement as a political issue. The atmosphere was extremely tense, and the community was frustrated with slum improvement promises from both major political parties, because neither party delivered on improvements in the past. At the same time, political actors used their party organizations to enrich their constituents. This unhealthy cycle of political wrangling jaded everyone's perspective and caused community members to generally dismiss external development programs as being driven for the purpose of securing votes for the coming election. But for the presence of a Catholic sister as the community liaison, the cross-sector collaboration process would have undoubtedly stopped at this point. However, because Catholic sisters are perceived with a high level of regard in Ghana due to their historic work with communities' most disadvantaged populations, Sr. Rita continued the interviews unimpeded. It was touching to observe the Muslim community members express themselves openly to the sister, although they had not met her prior to the survey, based on the historic relationship of trust between sisters and Muslim communities in northern Ghana.

A purposive sample of fifty-nine interviewees was selected in a snowball process. Many interviews lasted more than two hours and up to four hours. This was longer than expected, but the research team believed it was culturally appropriate. It seemed important to allow community members time to express their frustration with the slum conditions, their hopes and fears about working with the AMA, and their opinions about whatever else they wanted to discuss.

Interviewees expressed willingness to share their opinions mostly because they trusted the Catholic sister. Interviews were audio recorded and portions were later translated and transcribed or used for notes. By the end of the process, the interview team (Sr. Rita, Batsa, and Toyibu) believed they achieved saturation.

The NCHS Research Department entered the data using MS Excel 2013 and exported and analyzed it using SPSS version 16. Results were presented in the form of tables, charts, frequencies, and cross tabulation (bivariate analysis). The NCHS research team analyzed the survey responses to identify the most important elements, both positive and negative, that should be taken into account during the development of a latrine installation and management plan.

Areas of consensus, which are defined as when 100 percent of the interviewees "Strongly Agree" or "Agree" with the statement, were:

- The community should support sanitation management.
- Members of the community should actively participate in implementing sanitation management.
- It is the duty of community members to participate in and work with any program that involves community development.
- Overall it is nicer to work in a group than to work alone.

Although there was disagreement about many aspects of the project, the research director thought the areas of agreement were important for building shared understanding, and these were relayed back to the stakeholders through the PAR process. The PAR process provided a level of transparency and built trust among the stakeholders when they found that their opinions aligned with those of others.

Following the survey, the collaboration – in this case all of the stakeholder organizations, including Georgetown University, NCHS, Sr. Matilda's congregation the Handmaids of the Divine Redeemer, the AMA, the Catholic Archdiocese of Accra, and the Old Fadama Development Association – applied to the AMA for permits for two sets of twelve-seat latrines and two sets of four-cubicle bathhouses and accessories. As mentioned earlier, Sr. Matilda and Batsa served as key implementation partners, along with Boateng and the research director.

As noted, this research project did not have a budget for latrine installation. However, by this point, the stakeholders had contributed substantial resources to the PAR process: human resources (volunteer participation by all stakeholders), donated meeting space, and transport. The research team believed that this was an important step toward process sustainability, Collaboration Principle 6. These donations meant that funding was left in the research budget to begin latrine construction. The AMA donated latrine project costs, including design that included community input, architecture, budgeting, and permitting, all taking into account the challenging geography, flooding, and population density. Sr. Rita applied for additional funding to complete the project. These donations – first the human resources, then the project funds, then the successful application for funding – helped validate Collaboration Principle 5, that a process resourced with local funds contributes to stakeholder buy-in on the outcomes as well as to project sustainability, Collaboration Principle 6.

## 4 Confronting Development as Usual: Process and Project Results

The research focus on collaboration differentiated this project from typical international development programming. The community leaders and AMA representatives were receptive to this approach because they found that short-term projects did not ultimately meet their expectations or needs. Ghana's culture prizes education and academic endeavor, so the idea of participating in research that would be written up in academic publications was attractive to the participants. This interest in intellectualizing and modeling a process to create solutions seemed to be just as true for Old Fadama residents as for government officials. For example, one community leader who was not able to engage in the project for political reasons (unrelated to the project itself) tracked the effort for years, following the work through websites and academic conferences, before becoming engaged. Interestingly, the only participants who did not seem to care very much about research publication were the Catholic sisters, who believed that external communications had little bearing on their focus of concern for the poor, although this perspective did seem to shift over time.

The evidence from the literature review, incorporated into this PAR process as described in Section 2.4, contributed to the rigorous process. The use of mixed methodology including interviews, focus groups, questionnaires, and observations was consistent with the iterative nature of PAR. The high degree of contextual complexity incorporated into the research design was necessary for work on a volatile urban slum. Multi-level participation in the research, including nongovernmental organizations, grassroots community members, and government offices enriched the process and was necessary for latrine installation as will be described in Section 4.2.1. Capturing mechanisms, the often-unstated emotional reactions activated by the cross-sector collaboration intervention, was important to understanding the research participants' underlying needs and interests.

The creation of a rigorous PAR process yielded an unexpected benefit: the creation of trust between the research team and participants. The research team highlighted the research agenda as a mechanism for building transparency and created an understanding that the PAR process had an audience beyond those who were involved and those who were in Ghana. This transparency, coupled with continuous cross-checking and feeding data back to the research participants, became the cornerstone of relationships of trust. Many research participants expressed how it felt important to them that their opinions were collected, analyzed, shared with others, and built upon.

The results are organized by the two main themes that emerged. Section 4.1 describes the process results, including consolidating the collaboration principles and PAR process into a PAR intervention described in a flowchart. Section 4.2, project results, describes the sanitation strategy and latrine project development in further detail, with a focus on their impact on the PAR process. Additional information on the collaboration principles and how they helped to resolve process and project challenges are noted.

## 4.1 Process Results

The result of this concept phase is the PAR intervention described as a flowchart in Figure 10. The research team employed grounded theory to consolidate the collaboration principles, interviews, FGDs, and survey. The intervention includes outputs, outcomes, and impact described in Section 4.2.2: areas of focus that the research participants sought or occurred through the PAR process.

### 4.1.1 Collaboration Principles Results

This section explains further details about the collaboration principles (Figure 5), especially as to challenges that they helped the research team and participants overcome.

#### Complex Challenge

As Rittel and Webber (1973) and Heifetz (1994) have stated, understanding complex challenges comes through a deep knowledge of context, and the context is used to give the problem scope and to understand what solutions are possible. Consistent with the developed-country evidence from other contexts and cultures, in Accra, Ghana, this learning required considerable training. This shift involved complex psychological changes – as well as organizational and systems changes – as stakeholders realized that governments alone could not resolve these challenges.

The conceptual shift in the developed-country literature demonstrates the power of cross-sector collaboration as a dynamic learning process. The realities

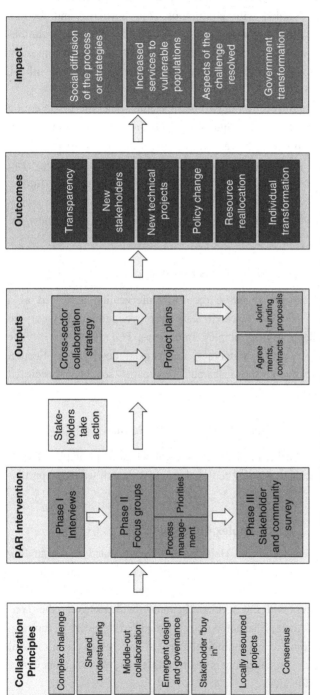

**Figure 10** Participatory action research intervention flowchart

of Old Fadama introduced massive political, social, economic, and environmental challenges – unpredictable in nature – into the PAR process mission and the stakeholders' learning around the real-world meaning of cross-sector collaboration in that context. Creating a "desirable difficulty" in training means introducing variation or unpredictability in the training process, which causes difficulty for the learner but enhances long-term performance (Bjork, 1994). In this project, Old Fadama seemed to act as the desirable difficulty, requiring deeper commitment of the stakeholders and collective better understanding of the challenge in order to collaborate and implement projects, leading to Collaboration Principle 1. Retrospectively, the slum – and the dynamics that created it and are causing its continued rapid growth – provided an extraordinary learning experience for both researchers and stakeholders.

## Shared Understanding

Shared understanding was necessary so that the complex challenge of Old Fadama could be broken up into a series of challenges for which the stakeholders – coming from their different fields and perspectives – could work as a team to design solutions based on the resources at their disposal or that they raised together. Shared understanding began in an interesting way. The research participants chose Old Fadama with the understanding that their own prior efforts there had failed. Boateng and the AMA failed to install latrines. Toyibu failed to bring needed development to Old Fadama when he was community secretary. Through many brief interviews with kayayei working in the markets, Sr. Matilda learned why they wanted to be in Old Fadama but failed to begin a project with the kayayei, even though she badly wanted to, because she could "not begin to touch the need" – it was so great. However, rather than being daunted by the information that others' prior efforts failed, this information seemed to energize the research participants. The shared knowledge created a shared perspective – even one about shared failures – that seemed to create enthusiasm. That, in itself, was an invaluable lesson for both researchers and stakeholders and led to Collaboration Principle 2. As the process unfolded and positive steps were taken, and more research participants became involved, the enthusiasm grew.

## Middle-out Collaboration

The project would not have continued, at times, without this new strategy of middle-out collaboration, Collaboration Principle 3. The sisters in the "middle" were an important example of bridging social capital (Woolcock &

Narayan, 2000). They proactively befriended each stakeholder to create relationships, trust, and respect. Their presence activated mechanisms such as enthusiasm, respect, and responsibility between the AMA staff and community members. One of the most powerful moments in the process occurred during the Technical Planning FGD when the lead sister prayed for those assembled to help their brothers and sisters in need. Another example occurred repeatedly during the survey data collection: community members frequently stated that they knew the project was a real effort, devoid of political influence, because a Catholic sister was involved. At that time, Old Fadama received frequent visitors from political organizations attempting to attract voters prior to the country's elections. Having a Catholic sister collect data differentiated this project, a long-term effort focused solely on the public good, from other politically motivated projects.

### Emergent Design and Governance

The Old Fadama collaboration employed emergent design and governance, which was consistent with the iterative process of the PAR intervention design. The research team believed that this approach was necessary given the continually shifting study context of a slum environment. There were several gaps in collaboration activity of a number of months, and one gap of six months when the research participants watched developments in the slum. For a typical development project, this would probably cause (or be considered) project failure. A predesigned process and timeline could never have planned for these gaps – due to critical issues such as flooding, elections, intertribal violence – in such a volatile environment. However, emergent design and governance allowed the research team and participants to wait when necessary and explore what was happening, creating a more rigorous process, with the result of Collaboration Principle 4.

Because of emergent design and governance, the research participants suggested additional research participants who joined the study when needed, based on the context. A few research participants did not continue to participate because their interests diverged with those of the project and others declined to participate. However, emergent design allowed the research participants to be selected with care, when they were essential, and they seemed to participate with that perspective in mind. By the end, the PAR process achieved the stakeholders' objectives and the project moved much more quickly than projected.

## Stakeholder Buy-in and Locally Resourced Projects

The prior evidence was that supporting distributed leadership and engagement requires financial investment in the cross-sector collaboration itself (Ali, Miyoshi, & Ushijima, 2006; Cancedda et al., 2014; Coppel & Schwartz, 2011; Thaennin, Visuthismajarn, & Sutheravut, 2012). Investment may include funds to link the collaboration to specific roles and responsibilities within organizations. It can also make funds available for project implementation to test the process, build relationships among the stakeholders, and work through organizational barriers. This project's initial approach was different: the idea was that a project that does not resource stakeholder participation or provide investment funds would require stakeholders to identify issues and goals central to their organization's own goals. The research director hoped that by creating a research project with no budget for human resources (other than the facilitator) or projects, the stakeholders would create a strategy that incorporated their own goals.

The hope was that fundamental change would cause them to make resources available from within their own organizations, which in turn would strengthen the collaboration. Because the community was accustomed to receiving payments or other consideration for participating in social development projects, at first it was challenging to create volunteer relationships. However, the positive results in this area were surprising. The project moved much more quickly than expected, resulting in unexpected cost savings that were reallocated to the latrine project. These learnings combined to make Collaboration Principles 5 and 6.

## Consensus

As demonstrated by this Element, the PAR process is incredibly time consuming. The facilitator must be trustworthy, committed, able to respond with openness to stakeholder frustration, and able to teach the rationale for cross-sector collaboration to stakeholders. Such a facilitator is key to the whole process. Batsa, this project's facilitator, was extensively trained – both at the outset and ongoing throughout the process – on the collaboration evidence base. A natural facilitator, he also trained as a project manager. This combined talent and skill set meant that he was able to achieve consensus at every step in the process. This goal was not discussed in the beginning. But, it was an aspect of the process that was, retrospectively, necessary in the conflicted context of Old Fadama.

### 4.1.2 PAR Intervention Results

The PAR intervention began with preliminary interviews that identified a location for the cross-sector collaboration, clarified the core challenges, and established the initial group of research participants – the initial stakeholders.

The interviews were used to identify themes that the stakeholders believed to be important, and local ideas and terminology helped to create a shared language for the collaboration and the unique roles and responsibilities of each stakeholder. The FGDs were used to identify community priorities and triangulate these priorities with government strategies. By feeding back the data into the FGDs, the community and government (and other) participants developed a shared understanding of the priorities that the collaboration should address. The FGDs were then used to create a sanitation strategy and latrine installation plan. The interviews and FGDs informed how the survey was designed around local concepts of shared responsibility and the importance of working together. The survey results reflected these concepts, which the research team believed validated the survey design. The stakeholders (listed in Section 3.3.3) thought that the survey results validated the latrine strategy and project design.

## 4.2 Strategy and Project Results

As described, the collaboration identified five community priorities based on the community chiefs' and leaders' definition of their own needs: sanitation, addressing community violence, supporting vulnerable kayayei, solid waste management, and building a clinic. The needs were triangulated with the government priorities, and the stakeholders created strategies and then projects to address each priority at its root cause. This section focuses on the sanitation strategy and the latrine project, and how they informed the PAR intervention impact.

### 4.2.1 Latrine Strategy and Project Results

Latrines were exciting for the community leaders because, as one of them said in FGD 2, "cholera is killing us today." Two aspects of latrine installation impacted the broader cross-sector collaboration process: (1) the creation of policy change and (2) the stakeholders' planning for latrine sustainability. As described, from the beginning of the Old Fadama project, participants from all sectors – government, nongovernmental organizations, community, and citizens – were interested in creating sustainable solutions. They explored different strategies to address the sanitation priority. After discussing portable latrines, it became clear that installing permanent public latrines was the most sustainable option. However, as noted, there was a city policy against upgrading Old Fadama. In September 2015, the facilitator and community liaison, at the request of the collaboration, entered into negotiations with the AMA to change city policy. Following the community survey, the collaboration filed an application for permits to install public latrines and bathhouses, formalizing the negotiation.

The permits required planning approvals from multiple AMA offices that reviewed the collaboration's latrine proposal. The approvals had the gradual effect of changing AMA policy to allow slum upgrading in Old Fadama. For five months, the director of public health, facilitator, and community liaison contacted various city offices in turn, seeking approvals on the latrine and bathhouse permits. Each office provided input and then directed them to a different office for a new approval. It appeared that no office wanted to give the final approval for the plan, as no one wanted responsibility for finalizing such a change to city policy.

Although intense and frustrating, this protracted negotiation served the important purpose of improving the longer-term planning for sustainability (Kritz, 2018). As the latrine proposal circulated from office to office receiving different levels of approval, stakeholders were called upon to identify and analyze key barriers to sustainability. For example, the government identified that Old Fadama was not included in city planning because the slum developed on city land that was set aside as a floodplain. This meant, as noted earlier, that resources needed to be reallocated for the planning. In addition, the gap in city planning in the past meant that there were no roads to accommodate sanitation waste pickup trucks, so they would not be able to enter the slum due to access issues. However, the community leaders explained how the city's partial demolition of the slum – which destroyed latrines and created a newly cleared area – presented an opportunity by creating space for the new sanitation facility, and also opening up an access road.

The Catholic sisters, known for their long-term attention to communities in need, identified the importance of doing "what the community wants," meaning that the project needed to respond to community requests if it were to ultimately achieve sustainability. The sisters have a long-held value of creating charitable networks to support communities in need. Thus, when funding was needed for latrine installation, the Catholic sisters were able to use their charitable networks to raise foundation funds to supplement the research funding that was reallocated to latrine installation.

The facilitation and research team from NCHS determined that community leaders from multiple tribes regularly engaged in destroying one anothers' infrastructure. For example, political leaders from multiple tribes had used the headquarters of the community association for years. However, after an election, it had been destroyed in an act of supposed political vigilantism to keep another political party from using the facility. This cycle of violence was attributed to political retaliation, but just as often these kinds of actions seemed to be a guise for other issues. Thus, latrine signage about the collaboration helped insulate the latrines from destruction (see Figure 11).

**Figure 11** Latrine block signage

**Video 3** Tribal leader involvement. www.cambridge.org/Kritz_2nd_edition

And finally, through the analysis required to receive approval from each government office, all stakeholders identified the absence of a maintenance culture in the government. Their implementation planning addressed this gap through a community survey that bolstered community leaders' knowledge of the cross-sector collaboration process, coaching them on how to take responsibility for various aspects of latrine management. The city donated the land, approved infrastructure investment, and finally entered a long-term public-private partnership with the stakeholders – represented by Sr. Matilda and Batsa as key implementing partners – to manage the latrines.

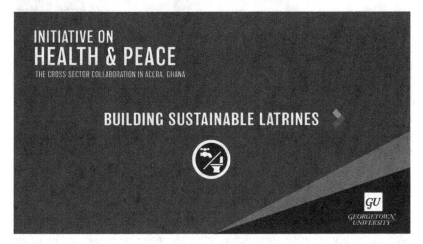

**Video 4** Building sustainable latrines. Video available at www.cambridge.org/ Kritz_2nd_edition

At the same time, other outcomes of the PAR process continued to develop, unbeknownst to the research team and participants. During the time that the research team shuttled from AMA office to office seeking the necessary permits, AMA employees discussed the proposal with their colleagues in Accra's sanitation business. As the business community took notice, the latrine project became a lively topic of conversation. The concept attracted the interest of multiple sanitation businesses that viewed the strategy as workable. They recognized a business opportunity.

The December 2016 national elections led to a new political administration with a specific policy and new ministry supporting slum improvement. Early in 2017, new AMA government officers expressed their gratitude for the collaboration's willingness to take on the challenge of sanitation in Old Fadama and immediately approved the stakeholders' latrine permits, formalizing the long-awaited policy change for Old Fadama slum improvement.

Having previously assessed the collaboration's proposal, the local sanitation businesses observed the city policy change and wanted to participate. This is

**Figure 12** Latrines installed by local sanitation business

where the research team discovered some surprising outcomes. As the cross-sector collaboration began latrine construction, other sanitation businesses, aware of the strategy, adopted the plans for latrine installation: on their own initiative and with their own resources, they began latrine construction in other areas of the slum. To date, six additional latrine and bathhouse blocks have been installed by local businesses (see Figure 12), investing their own resources and providing sanitation coverage in new areas of Old Fadama, providing another path toward local sustainability.

The strategic prioritization and planning process created a workable plan that external organizations eagerly adopted and began to implement on their own, to the benefit of the community. This was a very positive, yet unintended result for a community that had been so long frustrated with short-term projects led by internationally funded foreign investigators or collaborators. The previous projects resulted in time and resources taken from community members – but "nothing changed." Now all stakeholders could point to their own project results and community empowerment, having engaged multiple AMA offices and the community chiefs as well as survey participants in site selection and management. Over time, a local sanitation company was engaged to manage the latrines. While the latrine block is not yet a sustainable enterprise, the research participants believed that local sanitation businesses created a path toward sustainability on the broader issue of sanitation in Old Fadama.

## *4.2.2 Outputs, Outcomes, and Impact*

Cross-sector collaboration is personal to its stakeholders and thus can lead to different kinds of effects (Bryson, Crosby, & Stone, 2006; Innes & Booher, 1999; Moore, 1995). The outputs – concrete products of the PAR process – were straightforward and reflected the latrine project strategy and results.

## Outcomes

The research team collected data on outcomes the stakeholders sought. Knowing that collaboration outcomes are often surprising, the research team used thematic analysis to identify additional outcomes the stakeholders identified and valued (see Figure 10). Assessing the public value generated by collaborations often includes three dimensions: procedural legitimacy, democratic accountability, and substantive outcomes (Page et al., 2015).

Procedural legitimacy and democratic accountability were created through consensus-based decisions and a transparent process. Creating transparency in stakeholder positions and interests made it easier for stakeholders to develop shared understanding. Transparency was not a stakeholder goal but was retrospectively extremely important. The research team's continuous data collection, thematic analysis, and sharing of results with the stakeholders created transparency that held stakeholders accountable for their positions and decisions.

Between 2015 and 2017, stakeholders and organizations reallocated human and financial resources in order to work together. By 2017, numerous officials at several AMA offices were educated about the collaboration and they aligned their internal policies, human resources, and financing toward Old Fadama community improvement. The transparency made clear the time and effort it took for all stakeholders to reallocate resources and eventually create policy change. Stakeholders looked upon those steps with appreciation for the efforts made as well as the eventual outcomes. Continuous data collection on the position of the various government offices created democratic accountability: each public servant who gave input on the process was known, and their positions were understood by all stakeholders. The research team believed that using cross-sector collaboration to change policy in support of vulnerable populations was important in theorizing collaborative advantage in a low- and middle-income setting (see, e.g., Bryson, Crosby, & Stone, 2015; Emerson, Nabatchi, & Balogh, 2011; Innes & Booher, 2010).

Substantive outcomes during this time included more concrete and measurable outcomes such as enrolling new stakeholders and creating the latrine project. These outcomes indicated progress to the stakeholders and created enthusiasm.

Individual transformation was a fascinating outcome reflecting research on causal mechanisms that could either "advance or undermine effective collaboration" (Bryson, Crosby, & Stone, 2015). All stakeholders at times expressed similar strong emotions about the progress: excitement about the latrine project beginning, fear that politics and the upcoming election would interfere with progress, frustration with delays, and hope that they would be able to meet community needs. They persisted in the face of severe politicization of the community, such that every stakeholder felt this project had the strong possibility of severely negatively impacting their work and personal lives. These strong emotions, and the stakeholders' decision to persist – in fact without even seeming to consider ending the project – caused the research director to look for ways of explaining this transformation from a theoretical perspective. This analysis is explained in Section 5.3, Network Analysis.

## Impact

The developed-country literature defines impact as "the extent to which a cross-sector collaboration achieves its overarching and subsidiary purposes, meets applicable mandates, and achieves lasting and widespread benefits at reasonable cost that no single organization could have achieved alone in a democratically accountable way" (Page et al., 2015, p. 716).

In 2018, municipal government officials were ready to implement when overall sanitation infrastructure policy was changed. The causal chain of events can be described as follows. The stakeholders' latrine installation strategy created policy change to increase services in Old Fadama at a location where access was most limited. Social diffusion was demonstrated when local businesses began to participate by installing their own sanitation facilities, increasing sanitation coverage. This chain of events increased the public value the collaboration created and ultimately resolved the frequently reoccurring cholera epidemics.

The research team defined government transformation as organizational change that transferred the "lasting and widespread benefits" (Page et al., 2015, p. 716) from the collaboration to new projects, sectors, or settings. There were several examples of government transformation.

Lasting benefits were demonstrated in 2018, when political transition occurred and the community requested a meeting with the new AMA health director. He consulted the office records that indicated there were regular meetings with the Old Fadama community leadership. The new health director granted the meeting, discussed the community development agenda, thought the plans were reasonable, and supported community leadership to carry the plans forward to other offices. This series of events demonstrated that AMA's organizational change lasted between political administrations.

Widespread benefits were demonstrated in 2017 with regard to the stakeholders' second priority, community violence, a product of the generally lawless environment compounded by the slum serving as a harbor for violent criminals from throughout the city. Ghana's new president was elected and the research team learned he became increasingly frustrated about news reports on violence in Old Fadama. He directed his inspector general of police to address the issues. The deputy inspector general requested a meeting with Old Fadama community leaders and was told that they were unable to attend. Meetings with highest levels of police hierarchy were generally attended with alacrity so this response was a bit unusual and the deputy inspector general inquired further. He learned there was a prior meeting scheduled with the research director on latrine installation. He continued to learn more about the cross-sector collaboration – that it was going on for a number of years, the research purpose, and the novel PAR intervention. Another example of social diffusion: his conclusion was "this is something we can use." He surprised the research team, showing up at the latrine installation meeting accompanied by members of the media. The research director granted his request to use the stakeholder platform to begin a community policing program, if the community agreed. On the spot, in front of the assembled media, the deputy inspector general requested the community leadership to work with him to create such a program. He used the opportunity to educate the media and the community about the challenges of community policing, to build transparency by explaining the police hierarchy identifying the district office that would be in charge of the community policing effort, and to create shared accountability by asking the community chiefs, most of whom were assembled, to work with him on implementation. The police began working with the community. The facilitator and former AMA health director participated in a few initial meetings and then used this opportunity to observe what would happen if the process were not facilitated or tracked by the research team.

One year later, in 2018, the research team conducted interviews and observational research to see what was developed. The sixteen chiefs of Old Fadama were engaged by the district police office to appoint strong, ethical members of their tribes as community police. The number, including subtribes, meant that sixty-five community police were nominated and endorsed and subsequently trained on ethics and their responsibilities. Duties included volunteering information about criminal activity, organizing community cleanups, enforcing by-laws, and preventing and documenting crimes. While the community police donated their time, and did not have resources such as flashlights and whistles to facilitate their work, there was an exciting result: the slum was no longer a "no-go- zone." When crimes were identified, the government police force responded. By 2022, the process became a standard process for the district police agency.

## 5 Network Analysis: Replicating the PAR Intervention

In 2018-2022, the research team and core stakeholders replicated the PAR intervention around the vulnerable kayayei community members, who frequently experienced sexual violence and theft on the way home from work in the nearby Agbogbloshie market. The research focus was to see if and how new government sectors would participate, and to refine the intervention (particularly the outcomes and impact). The refinements are reflected in Figure 10 and incorporated throughout this edition of this Element. The research questions were:

1. Would new government stakeholders reallocate resources to new collaborations?
2. Was government policy changed?
3. Were services to vulnerable populations increased?
4. Did those services "resolve" aspects of the challenge to the stakeholders' satisfaction?
5. Would new stakeholders create the same organizational transformation?

**Video 5** Working with local NGOs on the issue of porter women (kayayei). Video available at www.cambridge.org/Kritz_2nd_edition

Available statistics from the registrar general's department pointed to the fact that more than seventy nongovernmental organizations registered to support Ghana's kayayei. However, the stakeholders perceived these organizations to have relatively little systemic impact. One particular example stood out. The head of the Kayayei Youth Association in Old Fadama attended a large, international conference focused on kayayei. He was excited to see there were nearly thirty internationally funded organizations representing their work, many of them in Old Fadama. He was a bit puzzled that he did not know about their work but very excited to become aware of new colleagues who shared his passion for supporting the kayayei. At the end of the day, he suggested to the conference organizers that they visit to see one anothers' projects. This idea was met with enthusiasm. Imagine his disappointment when only he and the conference organizers appeared the next day for the site visit. He concluded that no other "real" kayayei projects were at work in Old Fadama.

## 5.1 Phase I–II: Key Informant Interview, Focus Group Discussion, and Process Management Results

In 2017, through a purposive process, stakeholders identified a new research participant and implementation partner, Positive Action for Porter Girls, a community-based kayayei project in the Madina community, to work alongside the Kayayei Youth Association in Old Fadama. Creating programming was challenging for a number of reasons. Kayayei migrate back and forth between Old Fadama and their home communities, so programs begun in either location are frequently not completed. Kayayei endure the same challenging conditions as the rest of the community; however, their gender and their isolation from traditional family networks make them uniquely vulnerable. Due to the long hours they spend working, their children are often left unsupervised and cluster in groups around the slum.

Replicating the PAR intervention, the research team and participants conducted a series of interviews and FGDs to learn about the priorities of a purposive sample of one hundred kayayei identified by the Kayayei Youth Association and Positive Action for Porter Girls. The team learned that these women came to Accra with several priorities: health-care services, education for their children, and better economic opportunities.

Two FGDs were held with the sisters, the Kayayei Youth Association, Positive Action for Porter Girls, and technical officers from NCHS to explore possibilities for a strategy for addressing the kayayei community's challenges based on their priorities. The research participants identified three priorities and the facilitator and community liaison triangulated these with government priorities. Areas of shared priority were health (treating and preventing chronic and acute health conditions); economic (skill building and credit access); and education (education and social welfare of the children of kayayei). Stakeholders identified trafficking as an emerging issue.

In January 2018, three Catholic sisters (including Sr. Rita, the former community liaison) became facilitators. Coached by Batsa, they began to replicate the PAR intervention around the priorities to create new strategies to support the kayayei. The research team coached these new facilitators in an ongoing way, similar to the concept phase, on how to collect data to feed back into the PAR process and inform stakeholder decision making. These new facilitators and research participants – supported by the research team – began by identifying additional new stakeholders and inviting them to join the new cross-sector collaborations. At the outset, the research team taught new stakeholders how policy change occurred in the past and encouraged them to pursue this avenue.

In 2018–2019, stakeholders launched four projects in urban slums in Accra and Cape Coast, and eight projects in rural communities in northern Ghana.

**Video 6** Women of burden. Video available at www.cambridge.org/
Kritz_2nd_edition

**Figure 13** Kayayei at work

While the education, economic, and trafficking collaborations achieved similar government participation, the health sector in Ghana is larger and yielded more robust data on the health collaboration so it is reported here.

## 5.2 Health Project and Policy Results

The stakeholders' strategy, informed by concepts of social justice, was to provide comprehensive health services for each member of the kayayei community based on needs they identified. Aggregating the numbers of beneficiaries was challenging due to the community-driven design, which led to variability in services provided. The intervention, funded by this research project for 300 kayayei beneficiaries, included:

1. Conduct health talks educating the community about the need for screening and treatment;
2. Conduct community-based basic health screening and vaccination;
3. Identify treatment sites and connect kayayei to treatment for chronic and acute conditions diagnosed during the screenings;
4. Accompany kayayei to follow up care, using a trust fund supported by this project to pay for treatment as needed;
5. Enroll or re-enroll kayayei in insurance, as needed.

Many of the original one hundred kayayei key informants from 2017 migrated back to northern Ghana. So the sisters, Kayayei Youth Association and Positive Action for Porter Girls used a purposive process to identify new beneficiaries. Sr. Angelina Gerharz, SSpS, served as this project's facilitator, training and supporting officers from the Positive Action for Porter Girls. Nurses from the Catholic Health Guild, a new stakeholder, provided volunteer medical services. The project goals were immediately expanded to serve 940 kayayei when the local government polyclinic became a stakeholder, agreeing to provide test kits, reduced-cost vaccines, and screening and treatment materials.

The National AIDS Control and National TB Control offices and National Health Insurance Scheme (NHIS) were contacted, and they saw an opportunity to provide services to a population they were unable to reach. The facilitators were able to explain, based on the project's prior results, how policy change had happened before, and why it would be effective. These entities modified their policies in order to cost-share the setup for the screening. As the project expanded, government policy change included multiple steps described below. Due to health policy change, the collaboration expanded the number of beneficiaries from 940 to 1,534 kayayei.

The National Health Insurance Scheme (NHIS) was similarly invited to attend the screening and cost-share. Their financial policy was to engage in community-based enrollment when one hundred or more people could be enrolled or re-enrolled. The NHIS is a health agency and NHIS funds are put to work in the health sector. NHIS was enthusiastic about the volume of beneficiaries. However, funding for vouchers for indigent people to receive health insurance is administered by the Department of Social Welfare (DSW). DSW did not have funding to conduct community outreach. So, the collaboration paid for DSW to attend community health screenings and identify kayayei who could not afford health insurance. DSW screened these individuals and provided vouchers, which NHIS processed and the collaboration distributed to the kayayei in follow-up visits. Thus, rather than enrolling 300 kayayei, 1,789 indigent kayayei were enrolled in national health insurance in three locations – Old Fadama, Madina, and Ashanti Region.

Educated by the prior results of the intervention and coached how to make policy change, five government health agencies and the department of social welfare made policy changes including:

- budget allocation and reallocation
- service delivery adaptation: moving to provide services in the community itself
- modifying data collection processes accordingly

- working with collaboration stakeholders to incorporate the collaboration into government processes, creating accountability for staff follow-up
- increasing efficiency by deputizing stakeholders (Catholic Health Guild nurses, National Catholic Health Service research staff, and community-based organizations) to collect health and social services data.

The process replication continued, with new funding and a new target of 750 beneficiaries. By mid-2022, more than 10,000 beneficiaries received health services that they requested, thanks to the collaboration. Figure 14 visualizes the health stakeholders at the end of 2022.

In addition to direct services, community-based health provision provided lasting and widespread benefits regarding the stakeholders' 2015–2018 priority to build a clinic in Old Fadama. At that time, community residents felt unwelcome at nearby health facilities. As one community resident stated, "they think we are dirty and violent, and they don't want us there." So, the stakeholders created health access by conducting health programs in the community, accompanying beneficiaries on their follow-up visits to the polyclinic, and providing insurance and trust fund support where needed. This health intervention received substantial government investment, additional funds from a local charitable organization and later, international philanthropy. Thus, in 2019, when community leaders revisited the issue of building a clinic, the community itself deemed it unnecessary, reducing duplication and waste. This removed a major sticking point in the relationship between the community and the municipal government.

## 5.3 Network Analysis

As the PAR intervention created new collaborations, it was not possible to collect data from each group of stakeholders in the same exhaustive detail as during 2015–2017, leading to the idea of network analysis. In the United States, systematic research examined collaborative network activities among public organizations, making important contributions to the understanding of governance. Robert Agranoff's Managing Within Networks: Adding Value to Public Organizations (2007) provided a significant early step. He examined diverse sectors and employed grounded theory to describe and inform our understanding of how these interorganizational networks emerge, operate, and affect public problems. As public administration network analysis evolved, the field continued to focus on networks as a strategy to resolve public problems. The research focus continued to be placed on evaluating or describing networks in order to understand typology and effect (e.g., Provan & Milward, 1995).

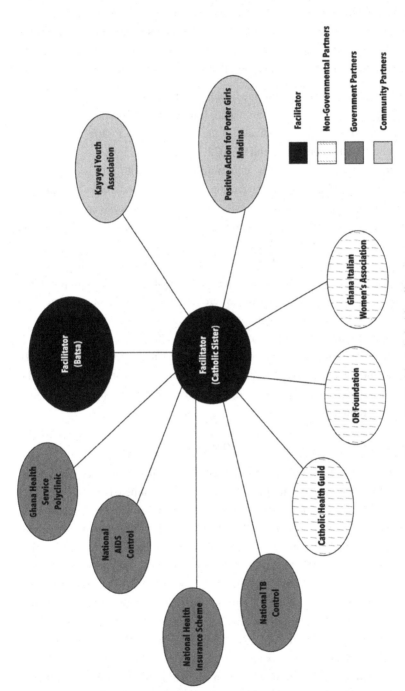

**Figure 14** Health stakeholder diagram

More recently, intervention research from public health was picked up by network analysts in public administration, who called for the field to expand upon the more evaluative or descriptive approach described earlier (Whetsell et al., 2020). Siciliano and Whetsell's scholarship harmonized the evidence, calling for public administration network analysis to incorporate the public health evidence on intervention, manipulating network mechanisms in order to achieve better network configurations to impact public problems (2021).

In 2015, the research director had a similar approach to this project, seeking to demonstrate how cross-sector collaboration evidence from developed countries could impact public problems in a developing country. To do that, the PAR process harmonized the public health evidence on intervention design with the robust cross-sector collaboration evidence from public administration. By 2020, the collaborations grew. The research team looked at network analysis as a way to visualize collaboration expansion, and understand why some collaborations were more successful than others. As Scott and Ulibarri (2019) point out, public administration studies focusing on institutional elements but lacking explicit network analysis can be categorized as "implicit network analysis." The research team took this perspective, looking retroactively at what developed in order to understand what factors were of interest to the stakeholders, in order to plan for network analysis as a potential tool to measure progress.

In 2018–2020, the new organizations and participants in the collaborations were straightforward, although the collaborations developed so rapidly it was challenging for the research team to keep track of all the new stakeholders. The research team employed grounded theory and similar methods to Agranoff's, moving beyond the social network evidence base into "network analysis" (2007, pp. 6–7) in order to incorporate not only the structure and operations of human networks but also issues of representation, formalization, and organizational effort. As reported earlier, the research team first reanalyzed the 2015–2017 collaboration, and validated and refined these results (which are reported in this second edition) with data from the PAR intervention replication in 2018–2022. The unit of analysis was each collaboration. Like Agranoff's subjects, the Ghana collaborations were substantively diverse including sanitation, microfinance, skills training, education, and health. Collaborations were both chartered (formally established through legal means) and nonchartered (not formalized under a legal construct) entities. Similar to Agranoff's methods, the research team's preparation for network analysis relied upon observation, document coding, and data from semistructured interviews and focus groups.

The more challenging aspect of the research was understanding the mechanisms that caused the collaborations to develop, expand, and provide services to vulnerable populations. In particular, the research director was interested in understanding the relationship change that precipitated cross-sector collaboration – the more appropriate configuration of stakeholders, such as Siciliano and Whetsell posited (2021). One key finding from Agranoff's work is that the value networks add to public management is context specific, often indirect, and not necessarily in keeping with traditional notions of outcomes. Measuring intangible and unpredictable outcomes is challenging (Peters, Gonsamo, & Molla, 2011). Measurements must be used to inform and build practice, improve efficacy, and contribute to openness and honestly through learning; this often takes place on a relational level (Taylor & Soal, 2010). These intangible benefits were explored to explain the pathway that was created from individual transformation to organizational transformation, when these new government stakeholders readily reallocated resources toward vulnerable populations.

Recent groundbreaking work on the psychology of democracy (Moghaddam, 2016) was helpful to explain stakeholders' individual transformation as they developed new skills working together. Moghaddam's study of the psychology of democracy built on a career studying intergroup relations, informed by living and researching the psychological foundations of democracy and dictatorship in countries with a variety of governance systems. He adopts a cultural psychology framework, which looks at human psychology through a rich holistic perspective on the relationship between an individual and their culture (see, e.g., Shweder, 1991). The research team felt this holistic approach was required to explore individual transformation in the context of this cross-sector collaboration intervention.

Moghaddam outlined ten critical convictions or behavior styles that guide the actions of a democratic citizen, represented in a circle diagram (Figure 15) because more than one can develop in the same time in the same person (2016, p. 51).

Analyzing the data through the lens of this diagram, it appears that the research team coached the stakeholders to develop skills for democratic actualization as follows:

- Stakeholders were reminded that they *could be wrong* through revisiting their prior individual approaches to Old Fadama that did not work. They were coached to actively listen to other stakeholders who had different perspectives on why they, too, failed in Old Fadama, and to be open to these different viewpoints.
- This approach led the stakeholders to *critically question everything* that they believed about Old Fadama in the past.

**Figure 15** Ten convictions of the democratic citizen

- They were coached to *revise their opinions when faced with new evidence*. As the research team repeatedly sought *information and opinions from different sources*, analyzed this data and shared the results in a continuous process, stakeholders realized they could *learn from those who are different from them*. At times, the facilitator coached them to reach consensus which meant that they had to *seek to understand those who were different*.
- Ghana is a religious culture, and meetings frequently begin and end with Christian and Muslim prayers. The sisters' prayers for each stakeholder to "help our brothers and sisters who are less fortunate" encouraged the stakeholders to be *actively open to the new experience* of the collaboration. As they developed shared understanding, stakeholders expressed that earlier feelings of being alone and overwhelmed at the challenges presented by Old Fadama were replaced by feelings of camaraderie that came from addressing the

challenges together. An example of a mechanism that was expressed repeatedly by all stakeholders at the individual level was transformation from not knowing one another, and often feeling at odds with organizational positions of other sectors, to feelings of friendship. These feelings were encouraged and supported by the Catholic sisters who, at the outset of the project, decided among themselves to try to build positive relationships between the stakeholders.

- This encouraged the municipal government to decide to *create new experiences with* the Old Fadama community, through designing strategies to impact community challenges.
- The idea that *there are principles of right and wrong* was brought to the forefront by engaging the sisters as moral leaders. They encouraged the stakeholders to *actively seek experiences of higher value,* such as deciding to install permanent latrines because they would be more sustainable and that is what the community had requested, even though this policy change was a more challenging route.

This exploration of principles from the psychology of democracy helped to explain how the PAR intervention was successful at building the stakeholders' skills to engage in collaboration and therefore participate in democratic governance, and the individual transformation the stakeholders experienced as a result of this activity. In 2018–2022, individual transformation created a welcoming environment for new collaboration stakeholders. The original stakeholders expressed kindness, enthusiasm, friendship, camaraderie, and gratitude. Over the years, these sentiments became norms that new government stakeholders adopted upon joining the collaboration. This shift will become the basis for network analysis in the next phase.

## 6 Conclusion

What happens when communities cannot solve the problems that most affect them, and individuals believe they are powerless? In Old Fadama, as in other places, the prevailing attitude at the start of the study was that "the government should fix it." Cross-sector collaboration led these stakeholders to embrace a different perspective. Prior to this PAR intervention, the AMA and Old Fadama community leaders were working together to accomplish discrete tasks, but without achieving the municipal government's planning goals or meeting community needs. However, attention to process, with the services of a research team, Batsa as a skilled facilitator, and Sr. Rita as community liaison helped create a shared language that reflected the cultural value placed on working as a team, which the survey demonstrated. The role of community leaders and the process of creating increased community participation were both important. The survey demonstrated that it was necessary to develop greater community trust in the government and understanding of Old Fadama's role in the collaboration to expand participation and create accountability for decisions. This shift was necessary for the community leadership to fully represent its own interests and assume the responsibilities of collaborative leadership in this challenging environment.

A limitation of this study was that the process was designed so that all study participants would perceive direct advantages of engaging in the collaboration, make an investment by resourcing their own participation, and ultimately benefit from collaboration, thus justifying their investment. Hence, the expectation or hope of continued support from the research team may have contributed to bias, in that the participants' responses may have been positively biased to attract further investment. The research team tried to limit this bias by clearly explaining the purpose of the study to participants and that the resources were limited to facilitation and research, requiring that the stakeholders make all decisions themselves. Probes were used to check answers for accuracy. In the beginning, responses were more positive, but as the process developed, the stakeholders were quicker to redirect the strategy or give feedback in disagreement with the research team and other stakeholders.

Other limitations, such as the qualitative nature of the study, the sample size, and the context-specific decision making by the stakeholders meant that it was not clear to us whether the model would be adopted elsewhere, or whether the PAR intervention could be replicated. The research team attempted to balance these limitations through a number of means. For example, interviews were believed to have reached saturation, indicating that interview numbers were sufficient to draw conclusions from the sample (Miles, Huberman, & Saldana, 2014; Patton, 2015). Consensus-based decision making in the FGDs served a similar purpose. Grounded theory was employed to try to capture the "truth" and therefore create results that are more generally applicable.

Now that the stakeholder platform has been replicated and expanded through social diffusion, results from more than fifteen locations and three government sectors lead to more general conclusions. Stakeholders and resources expanded rapidly, such that it was challenging for the research team to keep up. WhatsApp is widely used in Ghana, including by government representatives to communicate with colleagues. There is a WhatsApp Group for the original sanitation project, and for each new collaboration as it develops. Through WhatsApp, the research team, community members, and government officers – technical staff as well as ministry officials and even a Member of Parliament – communicate their ideas and observe policy change in real time.

Similarly, collaboration stakeholders and public servants meet as needed to discuss ideas, demonstrating that the stakeholders are applying their collaboration knowledge to new challenges, and organically providing this information to educate even more stakeholders. This means that collaboration has become part of organizational norms and operations of their organizations. As the process expands, it is possible to see how the work could be adopted or replicated in every slum in Ghana, as well as around other complex challenges or, as Rittel and Webber so memorably put it, "wicked problems."

At the beginning of the project, the Old Fadama community leaders shared numerous examples of international development failures in Old Fadama. Since then, it has been interesting to note how many stakeholders handle outreach from international development organizations. Stakeholders have long been aware of how international development projects persistently involve a sectoral approach and timelines that do not resolve complex challenges, with metrics that do not apply to stakeholders' highest priorities. Now, stakeholders have begun directing outreach from international development organizations to the research team. The research team is educating these organizations in the hope of helping them realign with the community's priorities. This realignment has begun to change the way international projects are viewed by the stakeholders themselves.

Almost always in the past, interventions in Old Fadama either failed or met with small, short-term success. This research affirms the importance of a stakeholder-driven, strategic approach geared toward resolving complex challenges at their root cause. Now, because of the stakeholder platform, the government collaborates there freely, using tools learned through this project – and in some cases, processes that their organizations incorporated that have now become an official part of government operations.

This work involves a novel approach. As new stakeholders join, the PAR intervention provides an adaptable guide for how to create strategies and projects based on existing resources and equips stakeholders with tested ideas on how to expand through collaboration, while retaining core values of the work. New stakeholders become part of a community of practice of colleagues with a long-term approach and careful attention to the evidence base on how to work together. In this way, the PAR intervention has become a project accelerator, combining new energy and ideas with the knowledge of the many people who are necessary to address complex challenges at their root cause. Based on their learning in the first phase, the facilitators and stakeholders employed the

PAR intervention even more rapidly and explicitly sought to attract new resources to meet community needs.

While an exciting development, this rapid growth is challenging to manage from a research perspective. Network analysis has been an important facet of developed-country collaboration research (Agranoff, 2007). The next phase of our project will involve network analysis of the growing collaborations, to understand the role of our new facilitators, the collaboration's growth into different geographic regions, and the way that stakeholders identify priorities and invest in strategies and projects. There is a gap in collaboration research that both employs rigorous theory and advances it, while also incorporating the rich material on process dimensions readily applicable to practice. This PAR intervention begins to fill that gap.

This ongoing research concludes that a small investment in cross-sector collaboration, facilitated through PAR, is a viable path to participation around urban slum improvement. The results from this project confront the development industry with a choice. Development agencies, researchers, and practitioners cannot continue funding and perpetuating outdated practices that are not effective and are no longer considered appropriate for complex challenges. Developing-country governments must adopt new solutions, such as this PAR intervention. This locally designed tool could be used to plan participatory processes in Ghana and other countries and may be applied to other challenges too complex for any one sector to resolve on its own or from the top down. Practiced in this way, cross-sector collaboration is a dynamic tool to address systemic issues in urban slums in developing countries worldwide. An African solution to African problems, this PAR intervention has become a grand strategy to resolve the grand challenges facing Ghana.

# Appendix A
## *Old Fadama Cross-sector Collaboration*
### Interview Protocol

Interviewee(s): _____

Date: _____

Interviewer: _____

Introduction

Old Fadama Collaboration
Purpose of project and our role
Confidentiality

## Introduction

1. [For first-time interviewees] Please describe your agency's role, and your personal role in deploying and operating programs in Old Fadama. [For repeat interviewees] Has anything changed in your agency's role or your personal role in Old Fadama since we last talked in [insert date]?

## Working Relationships/Collaboration

2. What are your current working relationships with the partner agencies in Old Fadama? Has this changed over the course of the Old Fadama cross-sector collaboration?
   a. [Let's get more specific] Who in the Old Fadama collaboration is making operational decisions?
   b. Who is making policies?
   c. Who has the power to decide how policies are made?
   d. And has any of this changed over time? [Prompt for specific examples.]

## Health

3. Health is a focus of the Old Fadama Collaboration. What role has health played in the overall Old Fadama Collaboration project? How have specific health-related issues been useful (or difficult) in your own Old Fadama work?

## Impact

4. From your perspective, what have been the immediate impacts of the Old Fadama collaboration? What impact do you foresee in the future? Have there been any negative impacts or outcomes from the Old Fadama collaboration?
   a. [Probe] Is this collaboration over [If not, ask about what may derail it in the future]? Will there be lingering effects?
   b. [Probe] One of the interviewees in our second year of research said, "There's no going back, we're going to continue working together across boundaries." Do you think this is still true? Can you provide specific examples of how this may or may not be true?

## End-user Impact

5. What do you think is the general public awareness and/or acceptance of the Old Fadama collaboration project? Has this changed over the course of the project's phases from planning to operational? How have your outreach activities contributed to the public's awareness and/or acceptance? What alterations have been made in the Old Fadama collaboration project as a result of user interaction with implemented systems?

## Wrap-up

6. Are there any other topics you would like to bring up related to the Old Fadama collaboration?
   a. Who else do you think we should interview?

# Appendix B
## *Old Fadama Cross-sector Collaboration*
## Focus Group Facilitator's Guide
### General Information

Date: _____

Location: _____

Number of participants: _____

Facilitator: _____

Assistant: _____

### Objectives

- Explore possible areas of cross-sector collaboration in Old Fadama
- Establish a theory of change for the collaboration
- Generate options for a collaborative project
- Assess awareness, access, and partnership capacities of each of the participants

### Introduction

At the beginning, set the scene: welcome people; explain the purpose and process; invite people to introduce themselves.

Provide some context: facilitate a brief initial discussion that is slightly broader than the Old Fadama collaboration. For example, begin by discussing the participants' work generally, or their organization in general.

This gives you a chance to warm people up to the important discussion to follow. It also provides you with an opportunity to learn how the group interacts. You can then plan your facilitation accordingly.

### Discussion

The purpose of this focus group is to develop a theory of change for our cross-sector collaboration. Theory of change unfolds through a facilitated process of open inquiry and dialogue. Participants may hold different views and perspectives but should share a broad commitment to change. The more the group reflects the voices of all constituents, the richer the dialogue is likely to be.

We want to imagine a vision of success. This is a short but specific picture in words of the sustainable future that we wish to help bring about. It describes real people, real relationships, institutions, and cultures. It is not a remote, idealized, and unachievable future. It must be a plausible picture of people behaving and experiencing life differently in a sustainable way that the organization, working alongside others, can meaningfully influence.

Use a general approach that begins with initial thinking. Follow that up with a discussion. Then ask people to extract themes from the discussion. Finally, ask people to interpret the themes to extract the meaning and significance.

From this kind of vision of what success looks like, the participants explore the question: What needs to happen to make this vision a reality? For each element of the vision, the participants try to identify ALL the prior changes that they think are necessary if the vision of success is to be realized – NOT just what the organization can do on its own. Slowly, a set of preconditions of success will begin to emerge.

Here are the steps:

- Explain the concept of the theory of change, and what you want from the discussion.
- Allow people a few minutes to think about their response to the concept or issue, without discussion. Suggest that they jot down brief notes of their ideas.
- [If people are slow to warm up, I follow the initial time for thought with discussion in pairs. Give the pairs a few minutes to get acquainted first. This enables people to "try out their words" in relative privacy before they have to express them publicly. It also helps to energize a reticent group.]
- Collect this information by going around the table, one person at a time. Ask people to listen to each other's contributions, identify themes, and note them down for the next part of the discussion or capture these ideas on a flipchart or whiteboard.
- Ask people to report the themes that they identified; capture these on butcher paper or electronic whiteboard (electronic whiteboards work well for this purpose).
- Facilitate a discussion on the relative importance and meaning of the themes. Capture the key aspects of this on butcher paper or electronic whiteboard.

## Wrap-up

From here, we will map the system in which we work. This involves understanding where we are now and then identifying all the actors in our system that can influence our vision positively or negatively. We can then consider what kind of working relationships we can build with specific actors that will help us achieve our vision more effectively.

- Solicit steps on the process moving forward.
- [If people are slow to respond, suggest a next step and solicit input on that step.]
- Thank participants.

# Appendix C
## *Old Fadama Cross-sector Collaboration*
## Community Survey (Sanitation Management)

### Objectives

- Understand opinions about community participation in cross-sector colla-boration for sanitation management
- Learn views about roles and responsibilities of community leaders and community members in cross-sector collaboration for sanitation management

### General Information

Date: _____

Name of participant: _____

Position of participant (i.e., organization, title): _____

Interviewer: _____

### Introduction

This interview is to understand your opinions about your role in cross-sector collaboration and sanitation management. We will start with some general questions and then move to specific questions about your opinions.

### About the Participant and the Community

1. Describe your role as [Position] at [Example Organization A]. What are your responsibilities? What are your activities? How do you interact with the cross-sector collaboration participants? How often?
2. Please tell me about a typical day in your life. What sort of work and activities are you involved in?
3. We will now discuss cross-sector collaboration and sanitation management. This is an important part of our process evaluation. It tells us whether we are creating relationships that benefit you. It also tells us how you see your role in sanitation management. You will answer a series of questions. Each statement has five options for answers: "strongly agree," "agree," "neutral," "disagree," and "strongly disagree." It is important to know any details that you want to share about your opinion on the statement so that we can make adjustments to the cross-sector collaboration process.

|  | Strongly Agree Agree Neutral Disagree Strongly Disagree |
|---|---|
| **Opinions about cross-sector collaboration with the community for sanitation management** | |
| Opinions about the usefulness of community participation in sanitation management | |
| Sanitation management should be supported by the community. | Strongly Agree Agree Neutral Disagree Strongly Disagree<br>Notes: [Prompt: How much should it cost to use a latrine?] |
| I have confidence in the skills of community members to support sanitation management. | Strongly Agree Agree Neutral Disagree Strongly Disagree<br>Notes: |
| I feel that local authorities want to work with the community on sanitation management. | Strongly Agree Agree Neutral Disagree Strongly Disagree<br>Notes: |
| **Views about the responsibilities of the community for sanitation management** | |
|  | Strongly Agree Agree Neutral Disagree Strongly Disagree |
| It is the responsibility of the community work together to support sanitation management. | Notes: [Prompt: In your family, who is responsible for sanitation management?] |
|  | Strongly Agree Agree Neutral Disagree Strongly Disagree |
| I can take action on my own to solve the sanitation problems of Old Fadama. | Notes: [Prompt: If you had $50 to spend on sanitation in Old Fadama, how would you spend it?] |
|  | Strongly Agree Agree Neutral Disagree Strongly Disagree |

(cont.)

| | Strongly Agree  Agree  Neutral  Disagree  Strongly Disagree |
|---|---|
| Members of the community should actively participate in planning for sanitation management. | Notes: [Prompt: What roles do the different people in your family – including men, women and children – play regarding sanitation management?] |
| Members of the community should actively participate in implementing sanitation management. | Strongly Agree  Agree  Neutral  Disagree  Strongly Disagree <br> Notes: |

**Opinions about knowledge of local authorities about sanitation problems and sanitation management**

| | |
|---|---|
| Local authorities are well aware of the health needs of our community. | Strongly Agree  Agree  Neutral  Disagree  Strongly Disagree <br> Notes: |
| Local authorities are well aware of the sanitation needs of our community. | Strongly Agree  Agree  Neutral  Disagree  Strongly Disagree <br> Notes: |
| Local authorities listen to my questions and my views about sanitation management and respond in a genuine way. | Strongly Agree  Agree  Neutral  Disagree  Strongly Disagree <br> Notes: |

**Views about leaders of community organizations in cross-sector collaboration and sanitation management**

Views on the role of the leaders of the community organizations in cross-sector collaboration

| | |
|---|---|
| Community leaders are fully aware of community needs for health and sanitation. | Strongly Agree  Agree  Neutral  Disagree  Strongly Disagree <br> Notes: [Do women and girls experience violence when accessing sanitation services in the community? Are there any structures in |

| | Strongly Agree | Agree | Neutral | Disagree | Strongly Disagree |
|---|---|---|---|---|---|
| | | | place in the community for addressing violence against women and girls? How does the community address violence against women and girls?] | | |
| I feel that community leaders are working sincerely and honestly for my benefit. | Strongly Agree | Agree | Neutral | Disagree | Strongly Disagree |
| | Notes: | | | | |
| Because of community leaders, I have more positive relationships with other people and organizations that can help my life improve. | Strongly Agree | Agree | Neutral | Disagree | Strongly Disagree |
| | Notes: | | | | |

**Views on the role of community leaders in sanitation management**

| | Strongly Agree | Agree | Neutral | Disagree | Strongly Disagree |
|---|---|---|---|---|---|
| Most community leaders are more concerned about their own welfare than the problems of the community. | Strongly Agree | Agree | Neutral | Disagree | Strongly Disagree |
| | Notes: | | | | |
| I feel that community leaders listen to my questions and my views and respond in a genuine way. | Strongly Agree | Agree | Neutral | Disagree | Strongly Disagree |
| | Notes: | | | | |

**Views on the need to pay leaders for participation in cross-sector collaboration**

| | Strongly Agree | Agree | Neutral | Disagree | Strongly Disagree |
|---|---|---|---|---|---|
| I have confidence and trust in the integrity of our community leaders. | Strongly Agree | Agree | Neutral | Disagree | Strongly Disagree |
| | Notes: | | | | |
| People who regularly serve the community deserve more than thanks. | Strongly Agree | Agree | Neutral | Disagree | Strongly Disagree |
| | Notes: | | | | |

| | Strongly Agree Agree Neutral Disagree Strongly Disagree |
|---|---|
| I feel that community leaders really care about me and want to help me as best they can. | Strongly Agree Agree Neutral Disagree Strongly Disagree<br>Notes: |

**Opinions about community participation in general, in cross-sector collaboration**

**Opinions about cross-sector collaboration, generally**

| | |
|---|---|
| I have the opportunities I need to tell the authorities what I want. | Strongly Agree Agree Neutral Disagree Strongly Disagree<br>Notes: |
| No program of community development can succeed without outside help. | Strongly Agree Agree Neutral Disagree Strongly Disagree<br>Notes: |
| It is the duty of community members to participate in and work with any program that involves community development. | Strongly Agree Agree Neutral Disagree Strongly Disagree<br>Notes: |
| I believe that the authorities will satisfactorily respond to and act upon my feedback. | Strongly Agree Agree Neutral Disagree Strongly Disagree<br>Notes: |

**Opinions about working together as a group**

| | |
|---|---|
| It is worth my effort to engage in cross-sector collaboration to try to get it to do what I think is important. | Strongly Agree Agree Neutral Disagree Strongly Disagree<br>Notes: |
| I feel completely free to ask questions and say what I really think in cross-sector collaboration. | Strongly Agree Agree Neutral Disagree Strongly Disagree<br>Notes: |
| Overall it is nicer to work in a group than to work alone. | Strongly Agree Agree Neutral Disagree Strongly Disagree |

|  | Strongly Agree | Agree | Neutral | Disagree | Strongly Disagree |
|---|---|---|---|---|---|
| **Views on the need to pay community members for participation in cross-sector collaboration** | | | | | |
| Most people in my community do nothing for free; you must give them something in return. | | | | | Notes: |
| The main reason to work with a community program is the benefits obtained. | Strongly Agree | Agree | Neutral | Disagree | Strongly Disagree Notes: |
| **Capacity of the community to work in cross-sector collaboration to solve their problems** | | | | | |
| The best way to plan and organize community activities is through community organizations. | Strongly Agree | Agree | Neutral | Disagree | Strongly Disagree Notes: |
| I feel that I am ready and willing to try new things offered by the cross-sector collaboration. | Strongly Agree | Agree | Neutral | Disagree | Strongly Disagree Notes: |
| I know that the more I put into cross-sector collaboration, the more benefits I will get. | Strongly Agree | Agree | Neutral | Disagree | Strongly Disagree Notes: |
| **Importance of community work, generally** | | | | | |
| Community organizations only delay the work because they spend time discussing things. | Strongly Agree | Agree | Neutral | Disagree | Strongly Disagree Notes: |
| I feel that I am ready and willing to try new things offered by cross-sector collaboration. | Strongly Agree | Agree | Neutral | Disagree | Strongly Disagree Notes: |
| I know that the more I put into cross-sector collaboration, the more benefits I will get. | Strongly Agree | Agree | Neutral | Disagree | Strongly Disagree Notes: |

# References

African Development Bank Group. 2012, *Urbanization in Africa*, Greenwood Press, Westport, CT.

Agranoff, R. 2007, *Managing within Networks: Adding Value to Public Organizations*, Georgetown University Press, Washington, DC.

Ahmed, S. A. & Ali, S. M. 2006, "People as partners: Facilitating people's participation in public–private partnerships for solid waste management," *Habitat International*, vol. 30, no. 4, pp. 781–796.

Airing, M. & Teegarden, B. 2012, "The billion dollar solution that isn't," *Development*, vol. 55, no. 1, pp. 71–80.

Ali, M., Miyoshi, C., & Ushijima, H. 2006, "Emergency medical services in Islamabad, Pakistan: A public-private partnership," *Public Health (London)*, vol. 120, no. 1, pp. 50–57.

Anderson, M. B. 1999, *Do No Harm: How Aid Can Support Peace – or War*, Lynne Rienner, Boulder, CO.

Ansell, C. & Gash, A. 2008, "Collaborative governance in theory and practice," *Journal of Public Administration Research and Theory*, vol. 18, no. 4, pp. 543–571.

Barnes, A., Brown, G. W., & Harman, S. 2016, "Understanding global health and development partnerships: Perspectives from African and global health system professionals," *Journal of Social Science & Medicine*, vol. 159, no. 10, pp. 22–29.

Bingham, L. B. 2009, "Collaborative governance: Emerging practices and the incomplete legal framework for public and stakeholder voice," *Journal of Dispute Resolution*, vol. 2009, pp. 269–547.

Bjork, R. A. 1994, "Memory and metamemory considerations in the training of human beings," in *Metacognition: Knowing about Knowing*, ed. J. Metcalfe & A. Shimamura, 1st ed., MIT Press, Cambridge, MA, pp. 185–205.

Brooke-Sumner, C., Lund, C., & Petersen, I. 2016, "Bridging the gap: Investigating challenges and way forward for intersectoral provision of psychosocial rehabilitation in South Africa," *International Journal of Mental Health Systems*, vol. 10: 21, pp. 1–15.

Brownson, R., Colditz, G., & Proctor, E. 2012, *Dissemination and Implementation Research in Health: Translating Science to Practice*, Oxford University Press, New York.

Bryson, J. M., Crosby, B. C., & Stone, M. M. 2006, "The design and implementation of cross-sector collaborations: Propositions from the literature," *Public Administration Review*, vol. 66, Special Issue, pp. 44–55.

2015, "Designing and implementing cross-sector collaborations: Needed and challenging," *Public Administration Review*, vol. 75, no. 5, pp. 647–663.

Bryson, J. M., Crosby, B. C., Stone, M. M., & Saunoi-Sandgren, E. 2011a, *Designing and Strategically Managing Cross-Sector Collaborations Propositions from the Literature and Three Longitudinal Studies*, 7th Transatlantic Dialogue on Strategic Management of Public Organizations, Rutgers University, New Brunswick, NJ.

Bryson, J. M., Crosby, B. C., Stone, M., Saunoi-Sandgren, E., & Imboden, A. 2011b, *The Urban Partnership Agreement: A Comparative Study of Technology and Collaboration in Transportation Policy Implementation*, Intelligent Transportation Systems Institute, Minneapolis, MN.

Campbell, C., Nair, Y., & Maimane, S. 2007, "Building contexts that support effective community responses to HIV/AIDS: A South African case study," *American Journal of Community Psychology*, vol. 39, no. 3, pp. 347–363.

Cancedda, C., Farmer, P. E., Kyamanywa, P. et al 2014, "Enhancing formal educational and in-service training programs in rural Rwanda: A partnership among the public sector, a nongovernmental organization, and academia," *Academic Medicine: Journal of the Association of American Medical Colleges*, vol. 89, no. 8, pp. 1117–1124.

Carpenter, A. C. 2019, "The role of conflict resolution in a major urban partnership to fight human trafficking," *Conflict Resolution Quarterly*, vol. 36, no. 4, pp. 311–327.

Carrington, P. J., Scott, J., & Wasserman, S. 2005, *Models and Methods in Social Network Analysis*, Cambridge University Press, Cambridge.

Coppel, G. P. & Schwartz, K. 2011, "Water operator partnerships as a model to achieve the Millenium Development Goals for water supply? Lessons from four cities in Mozambique," *Water SA*, vol. 37, no. 4, p. 575–583.

Cornwall, A. & Jewkes, R. 1995, "What is participatory research?" *Social Science & Medicine*, vol. 41, no. 12, pp. 1667–1676.

Dart, J. & Davies, R. 2003, "A dialogical, story-based evaluation tool: The most significant change technique," *American Journal of Evaluation*, vol. 24, no. 2, pp. 137–155.

Duff, J. F. & Buckingham, W. W. 2015, "Strengthening of partnerships between the public sector and faith-based groups," *The Lancet*, vol. 386, no. 10005, pp. 1786–1794.

Easterly, W. R. 2008, *Re-inventing Foreign Aid*, MIT Press, Cambridge, MA.

Emerson, K., Nabatchi, T., & Balogh, S. 2011, "An integrative framework for collaborative governance," *Journal of Public Administration Research and Theory*, vol. 22, no. 1, pp. 1–29.

Eyben, R. 2010, "Hiding t-relations: The irony of effective aid," *European Journal of Development Research*, vol. 22, pp. 382–397.

Fagence, M. 2014, *Citizen Participation in Planning*, 19th ed., Elsevier, New York.

Farouk, B. R. & Owusu, M. 2012, "'If in doubt, count': The role of community-driven enumerations in blocking eviction in Old Fadama, Accra," *Environment & Urbanization*, vol. 24, no. 1, pp. 47–57.

Festinger, L. 1962, *A Theory of Cognitive Dissonance*, Stanford University Press, Stanford, CA.

Flint, A. & zu Natrup, C. M. 2019, "Aid and development by design: Local solutions to local problems," *Development in Practice*, vol. 29, no. 2, pp. 208–219.

Fowler, A. 2000, "NDGOs as a moment in history," *Third World Quarterly*, vol. 21, no. 4, pp. 637–654.

2001, *The Virtuous Spiral: A Guide to Sustainability for NGOs in International Development*, Earthscan, London.

Friere, P. 2013, *Pedagogy of the Oppressed*, 30th Anniversary ed. Bloomsbury, New York.

Greenwood, D. J. & Levin, M. 1998, *Introduction to Action Research*, Sage, Thousand Oaks, CA.

Gruen, R. L., Elliott, J. H., Nolan, M. L. et al 2008, "Sustainability science: An integrated approach for health-programme planning," *The Lancet*, vol. 372, no. 9649, pp. 1579–1589.

Heifetz, R. A. 1994, *Leadership without Easy Answers*, Belknap Press of Harvard University, Cambridge, MA.

Innes, J. E. & Booher, D. E. 1999, "Consensus building and complex adaptive systems: A framework for evaluating collaborative planning," *Journal of the American Planning Association*, vol. 65, no. 4, pp. 412–423.

2010, *Planning with Complexity: An Introduction to Collaborative Rationality for Public Policy*, Routledge, New York.

Kapiriri, L., Ole Frithjof, N., & Kristian, H. 2003, "Public participation in health planning at the district level in Uganda," *Journal of Health Policy and Planning*, vol. 18, no. 2, pp. 205–213.

Kielmann, K., Datye, V., Pradhan, A., & Rangan, S. 2014, "Balancing authority, deference and trust across the public-private divide in health care: Tuberculosis health visitors in western Maharashtra, India," *Global Public Health*, vol. 9, no. 8, pp. 975–992.

Kritz, J. 2017, "A realist systematic review of cross-sector collaboration implementation in developing countries & mediation as a useful instrument," *Pepperdine Dispute Resolution Law Journal*, vol. 17, no. 369, pp. 369–403.

2018, "Effective cross-sector collaborations create sustainability," *The Lancet Global Health*, vol. 6, no. 9, pp. e952–e953.

Kritz, J. & Moghaddam, F. 2018, "Cross-sector collaboration: A tool for democratic health policy transformation," *American Journal of Public Health*, vol. 108, no. 6, pp. 739–740.

Laumann, E., Galaskiewicz, J., & Marsden, P. 1978, "Community structure as interorganizational linkages," *Annual Review of Sociology*, vol. 4, p. 455–484.

Li, B., Huikuri, S., Zhang, Y., & Chen, W. 2015, "Motivating intersectoral collaboration with the Hygienic City Campaign in Jingchang, China," *Environment & Urbanization*, vol. 27, no. 1, pp. 285–302.

Magrab, P. R. & Raper, J. 2010, "Building strategic relationships," in *The Leadership Equation: Strategies for Individuals Who Are Champions for Children, Youth, and Families*, ed. G. M. Blau & P. R. Magrab, Brookes, Baltimore, MD, pp. 87–98.

Maluka, S. O. 2011, "Strengthening fairness, transparency and accountability in health care priority setting at district level in Tanzania," *Global Health Action*, vol. 4, no. 1, pp. 1–11.

Manning, S. & Roessler, D. 2014, "The formation of cross-sector development partnerships: How bridging agents shape project agendas and longer-term alliances," *Journal of Business Ethics*, vol. 123, no. 3, pp. 527–547.

Marsden, P. 1990, "Network and data measurement," *Annual Review of Sociology*, vol. 16, pp. 435–463.

Martin, P. Y. & Turner, B. A. 1986, "Grounded theory and organizational research," *The Journal of Applied Behavioral Science*, vol. 22, no. 2, pp. 141–157.

Mathie, A. & Cunningham, G. 2003, "From clients to citizens: Asset-based community development as a strategy for community-driven development," *Development in Practice*, vol. 13, no. 5, pp. 474–486.

Miles, M. B., Huberman, A. M., & Saldana, J. 2014, *Qualitative Data Analysis: A Methods Sourcebook*, 3rd ed., Sage, Newbury Park, CA.

Mintzberg, H., Ahlstrand, B., & Lampel, J. 1998, *Strategy Safari: A Guided Tour through the Wilds of Strategic Management*, 1st ed., Free Press, New York.

Moghaddam, F. M. 2016, *The Psychology of Democracy*, American Psychological Association, Washington, DC.

Moore, M. H. 1995, *Creating Public Value*, Harvard University Press, Cambridge, MA.

Moyo, D. 2010, *Dead Aid: Why Aid Is Not Working and How There Is a Better Way for Africa*, Farrar, Straus and Giroux, New York.

Murthy, K. J. R., Frieden, T. R., Yazdani, A., & Hreshikesh, P. 2001, "Public-private partnership in tuberculosis control: Experience in Hyderabad, India," *The International Journal of Tuberculosis and Lung Disease*, vol. 5, no. 4, pp. 354–359.

Ostrom, E. 1990, *Governing the Commons: The Evolution of Institutions for Collective Action*, Cambridge University Press, New York.

2014, *Choice, Rules, and Collective Action: The Ostroms on the Study of Institutions and Governance*, ECPR Press, Colchester.

Page, S. B., Stone, M. M., Bryson, J. M., & Crosby, B. C. 2015, "Public value creation by cross-sector collaborations: A framework and challenges of assessment," *Public Administration*, vol. 93, no. 3, pp. 715–732.

Paller, J.W. 2014, "Informal institutions and personal rule in urban Ghana," *African Studies Review*, vol. 57, no. 3, pp. 123–142.

2015, "Informal networks and access to power to obtain housing in urban slums in Ghana," *Africa Today*, vol. 62, no. 1, pp. 31–55.

2019, *Democracy in Ghana: Everyday Politics in Urban Africa*, Cambridge University Press, Cambridge.

Patten, S., Mitton, C., & Donaldson, C. 2006, "Using participatory action research to build a priority setting process in a Canadian Regional Health Authority," *Social Science & Medicine*, vol. 63, no. 5, pp. 1121–1134.

Patton, M. Q. 2015, *Qualitative Research and Evaluation Methods: Integrating Theory and Practice*, 4th ed., Sage, Newbury Park, CA.

Pawson, R., Greenhalgh, T., Harvey, G., & Walshe, K. 2005, "Realist review: A new method of systematic review designed for complex policy interventions," *Journal of Health Services Research & Policy*, vol. 10, no. 1 suppl., pp. 21–34.

Pawson, R. & Tilley, N. 1997, *Realistic Evaluation*, Sage, London.

Peters, B., Gonsamo, M., & Molla, S. 2011, "Capturing unpredictable and intangible change: Evaluating asset-based community development (ABCD) approach in Ethiopia," *Coady International Institute Occasional Paper Series*, vol. 10.

Peters, D., Adam, T., Alonge, O., Agyepong, I., & Tran, N. 2013, "Implementation research: What it is and how to do it," *British Medical Journal*, vol. 347, no. f6793, pp. 1–7.

Pridmore, P., Carr-Hill, R., Amuyunzu-Nyamongo, M. et al. 2015, "Tackling the urban health divide though enabling intersectoral action on malnutrition in Chile and Kenya," *Journal of Urban Health*, vol. 92, no. 2, pp. 313–321.

Probandari, A., Utarini, A., Lindholm, L., & Hurtig, A. 2011, "Life of a partnership: The process of collaboration between the National Tuberculosis Program and the hospitals in Yogyakarta, Indonesia," *Social Science & Medicine*, vol. 73, no. 9, pp. 1386–1394.

Provan, K. G. & Milward, H. B. 1995, "A preliminary theory of interorganizational network effectiveness: A comparative study of four community mental health systems," *Administrative Science Quarterly*, vol. 40, no. 1, pp. 1–33.

Ramiah, I. & Reich, M. R. 2006, "Building effective public–private partnerships: Experiences and lessons from the African Comprehensive HIV/AIDS Partnerships (ACHAP)," *Social Science & Medicine*, vol. 63, no. 2, pp. 397–408.

Rangan, S. G., Juvekar, S. K., Rasalpurkar, S. B. et al 2004, "Tuberculosis control in rural India: Lessons from public-private collaboration," *The International Journal of Tuberculosis and Lung Disease*, vol. 8, no. 5, pp. 552–559.

Rittel, H. W. J. & Webber, M. M. 1973, "Dilemmas in a general theory of planning," *Policy Sciences*, vol. 4, no. 2, pp. 155–169.

Saadé, C., Bateman, M., & Bendahmane, D. B. 2001, *"The Story of a Successful Public-Private Partnership in Central America: Handwashing for Diarrheal Disease Prevention*, Basic Support for Child Survivial Project (Basics II), Environmental Health Project, UNICEF, USAID, and the World Bank, Arlington, VA

Sablah, M., Klopp, J., Steinberg, D. et al. 2012, "Thriving public-private partnership to fortify cooking oil in the West African Economic and Monetary Union (UEMOA) to control vitamin A deficiency: Faire Tache d'Huile en Afrique de l'Ouest," *Food and Nutrition Bulletin*, vol. 33, no. 4 suppl., p. 310–320.

Sachs, J. 2006, *The End of Poverty: Economic Possibilities for Our Time*, Penguin Books, New York.

Sanchez, L., Perez, D., Cruz, G. et al. 2009, "Intersectoral coordination, community empowerment and dengue prevention: Six years of controlled interventions in Playa Municipality, Havana, Cuba," *Tropical Medicine & International Health*, vol. 14, no. 11, pp. 1356–1364.

Sanchez, L., Perez, D., Pérez, T. et al. 2005, "Intersectoral coordination in *Aedes aegypti* control. A pilot project in Havana City, Cuba," *Tropical Medicine & International Health*, vol. 10, no. 1, pp. 82–91.

Scott, T. A. & Ulibarri, N. 2019, "Taking network analysis seriously: Methodological improvements for governance network scholarship," *Perspectives on Public Management and Governance*, vol. 2, no. 2, pp. 89–101 https://doi.org/10.1093/ppmgov/gvy011.

Shediac-Rizkallah, M. C. & Bone, L. R. 1998, "Planning for the sustainability of community-based health programs: Conceptual frameworks and future directions for research, practice and policy," *Health Education Research*, vol. 13, no. 1, pp. 87–108.

Shweder, R. 1991, *Thinking through Cultures: Expeditions in Cultural Psychology*, Harvard University Press, Cambridge, MA.

Siciliano, M. D. & Whetsell, T. A. 2021, "Strategies of network intervention: A pragmatic approach to policy implementation and public problem resolution through network science," *arXiv preprint, arXiv: 2109.08197*.

Spiegelman, D. 2016, "Evaluating public health interventions: 1. Examples, definitions, and a personal note," *American Journal of Public Health*, vol. 106, no. 1, pp. 70–73.

Stone, M., Crosby, B., & Bryson, J. 2013, "Adaptive governance in collaborations," in *Nonprofit Governance: Innovative Perspectives and Approaches*, ed. C. Cornforth & W. Brown, Routledge, New York, pp. 249–271.

Stringer, E. T. 1999, *Action Research*, 2nd ed., Sage, Thousand Oaks, CA.

Taylor, J. & Soal, S. 2010, "Measurement in development practice: From the mundane to the transformational," in *NGO Management: An Earthscan Companion*, ed. A. Fowler & C. Malung, Earthscan, Washington, DC, pp. 321–335.

Thaennin, N., Visuthismajarn, P., & Sutheravut, P. 2012, "Participation in agri-food safety collaborative network: An example from Songkhla Province, Thailand," *International Journal of Management & Information Systems (IJMIS)*, vol. 16, no. 4, p. 331–339.

Thomson, A. M. & Perry, J. L. 2006, "Collaboration processes: Inside the black box," *Public Administration Review*, vol. 66, Special Issue, pp. 20–32.

United Nations Human Settlement Program. 2006, *State of the World's Cities 2006/2007*, Earthscan in the UK and USA on behalf of the United Nations Human Settlements Programme (UN-HABITAT), Nairobi, Kenya.

United Nations Statistics Division, Department of Economic and Social Affairs. 2014a, *Millennium Development Goals Indicators: Slum Population as Percentage of Urban, Percentage*, United Nations, New York.

2014b, *Millennium Development Goals Indicators: Slum Population in Urban Areas (Thousands)*, United Nations, New York.

Wallerstein, N. & Duran, B. 2010, "Community-based participatory research contributions to intervention research: The intersection of science and practice to improve health equity," *American Journal of Public Health*, vol. 100, pp. S4–S46.

Wessells, M. G. 2015, "Bottom-up approaches to strengthening child protection systems: Placing children, families, and communities at the center," *Child Abuse & Neglect*, vol. 43, pp. 8–21.

Whetsell, T. A., Siciliano, M. D., Witkowski, K. A., & Leiblein, M. J. 2020, "Government as network catalyst: Accelerating self-organization in a strategic industry," *Journal of Public Administration Research and Theory*, vol. 30, no. 3, pp. 448–464. https://doi.org/10.1093/jopart/muaa002.

Woolcock, M. & Narayan, D. 2000, "Social capital: Implications for theory, research, and policy," *The World Bank Research Observer*, vol. 15, no. 2, pp. 225–249.

World Health Organization. 2019, "Health as bridge for peace." www.who.int /hac/techguidance/hbp/en/.

# Acknowledgments

This participatory action research was made possible with funding from the Conrad N. Hilton Foundation. The foundation, researchers, and stakeholders shared an agenda of reaching the most vulnerable and disadvantaged. The foundation's appreciation for long-term outcomes and value placed on collaboration as a means to achieve them offered an unusual level of flexibility during the concept phase. This approach allowed researchers to enter a conflicted environment, engage Catholic sisters as agents for change to build bridges between the government and community, and empower all stakeholders to create a locally driven model for change. A strategic funding partner, the foundation offered the opportunity in the pilot phase to expand based on stakeholder needs and interests. The views expressed are those of the author, not the stakeholders, research participants, or funder.

When approached about this project, Dr. Simpson A. Boateng, director of public health of the Accra Metropolitan Assembly (2007–16) said words I will never forget:

> Thank God you are here. We need help. Everything we have tried in this community seems to fail. I am meeting with the press again this morning about the cholera epidemic that originated there. We can't find the solution to this problem on our own. I am willing to try anything.

Dr. Boateng passed away on January 21, 2019. Until the month of his death, he was a tireless advocate for this project and the possibilities it created for Ghana. It was a pleasure and an honor to work with him.

The stakeholder platform exists, first and foremost, thanks to the efforts of our talented, committed facilitator Peter N. Batsa, who leads the research team in Accra, and our steady, skilled community liaison, Sr. Rita Ann Kusi, H.D.R. My deepest thanks to George Adjei, director of the National Catholic Health Service, who identified Sr. Matilda Sorkpor, H.D.R., as the first stakeholder. Imoro Toyibu, the Department of Public Health's officer-in-charge for Old Fadama, was essential to bringing community leaders to the table.

The most challenging aspect of this research, in the concept phase, was repeatedly realizing what a herculean task we had undertaken. Feeling alone was never a problem: so many, many stakeholders and research participants, too numerous to mention, are working every day to build understanding and make the world a better place, and they have taken the time to educate me and one another, to the benefit our project. Ghana owes you a debt of gratitude, as do I.

On the Washington, DC, side, a big thank you to Jessica Bissett and Claire Anderson for invaluable project management. Video is an essential tool for communicating complexity. The video benefited greatly from the interventions of Mahiely and Bokeem Woodbine on storytelling and narration, and Tim Casey and the Case Communications team on video production. Audra Gold provided critical consultation on global health publications and presentations. The political aspects of the project would not have been so effectively managed without consultation with Jesse Boateng on Ghana politics.

Words cannot express my gratitude to editor Chris Harrison at Cambridge University Press for this important new Elements format. Series editors Robert Christensen and Andrew Whitford provided invaluable professional advice and assistance in conveying this diffuse project.

Thank you to colleagues Howard J. Federoff, Joseph Ferrara, Robert Burkett, Bernhard Liese, Victoria Jennings, Fathali M. Moghaddam. and Dominick Shattuck for their support, especially early in the project. Many thanks to colleague John Palguta for incisive comments on a draft of the manuscript, and Carole Sargent for editorial guidance throughout the project. Thanks to Craig Zelizer, Catalina Rojas-Zelizer, Douglas Irvin-Erickson, and Molly Inman, for their comments on drafts of earlier works leading to this Element.

Many thanks for countless hours of work from research assistants Arianne Malekzadeh, Evan Tueller, Jessica Bissett, Kate Scoczalek and Georgia Garney.

And a very special thank you to my husband, Brian Kritz, for endless support, lending a lawyer's careful eye throughout the project, and beautifully managing things when I was conducting field research; and to our son, Theodore, whose boundless energy and enthusiasm is a joy to behold, and a reminder to always step back and look at the big picture.

## Cambridge Elements ≡

# Public and Nonprofit Administration

## Andrew Whitford

*University of Georgia*

Andrew Whitford is Alexander M. Crenshaw Professor of Public Policy in the School of Public and International Affairs at the University of Georgia. His research centers on strategy and innovation in public policy and organization studies.

## Robert Christensen

*Brigham Young University*

Robert Christensen is Professor and George Romney Research Fellow in the Marriott School at Brigham Young University. His research focuses on prosocial and antisocial behaviors and attitudes in public and nonprofit organizations.

### About the Series

The foundation of this series are cutting-edge contributions on emerging topics and definitive reviews of keystone topics in public and nonprofit administration, especially those that lack longer treatment in textbook or other formats. Among keystone topics of interest for scholars and practitioners of public and nonprofit administration, it covers public management, public budgeting and finance, nonprofit studies, and the interstitial space between the public and nonprofit sectors, along with theoretical and methodological contributions, including quantitative, qualitative, and mixed-methods pieces.

### The Public Management Research Association

The Public Management Research Association improves public governance by advancing research on public organizations, strengthening links among interdisciplinary scholars, and furthering professional and academic opportunities in public management.

Cambridge Elements ≡

# Public and Nonprofit Administration

## Elements in the Series

*Trust in Government Agencies in the Time of COVID-19*
Scott E. Robinson, Kuhika Gupta, Joseph Ripberger, Jennifer A. Ross, Andrew Fox,
Hank Jenkins-Smith and Carol Silva

*Partnership Communities: Public-Private Partnerships and Non-Market
Infrastructure Development Around the World*
Anthony Michael Bertelli, Eleanor Florence Woodhouse, Michele Castiglioni and
Paolo Belardinelli

*Shared Measures: Collective Performance Data Use in Collaborations*
Alexander Kroll

*Critical Race Theory: Exploring Its Application to Public Administration*
Norma M. Riccucci

*Rage Giving*
Jennifer A. Taylor and Katrina Miller-Stevens

*Apples to Apples: A Taxonomy of Networks in Public Management and Policy*
Branda Nowell and H. Brinton Milward

*Country Size and Public Administration*
Marlene Jugl

*Contingent Collaboration: When to Use Which Models for Joined-up Government*
Rodney J. Scott and Eleanor R. K. Merton

*The Hidden Tier of Social Services: Frontline Workers' Provision of Informal
Resources in the Public, Nonprofit, and Private Sectors*
Einat Lavee

*Networks in the Public Sector: A Multilevel Framework and Systematic Review*
Michael D. Siciliano, Weijie Wang, Qian Hu, Alejandra Medina and David
Krackhardt

*Public Administration and Democracy: The Complementarity Principle*
Anthony M. Bertelli and Lindsey J. Schwartz

*Redefining Development: Resolving Complex Challenges in a Global Context*
(Second Edition)
Jessica Kritz

A full series listing is available at: www.cambridge.org/EPNP

Printed in the United States
by Baker & Taylor Publisher Services